HOLY SHIFT!

A NO NONSENSE GUIDE TO STOP FRONTING
AND EMBODY THE PERSON YOU WERE
MEANT TO BE.

LINDSEY CURRY

ISBN: 978-1-950621-09-5 (Paperback)

ISBN: 978-1-950621-07-1 (Ebook)

ISBN: 978-1-950621-08-8 (Hardcover)

Published by LightHouse Global Publishing and PR LLC

www.lighthouseglobalinc.com

For my daughters, Bella, Maryn & Ardyn.

This is a manifesto of my truth and your motherly nudge to embody yours, always.
-Mama

CONTENTS

Your authentic self is
your secret sauce.
-Lindsey

WELCOME TO THE SHIT SHOW CIRCUS

Everyone can list one thing in their life that they can shift to free themselves from unnecessary stress. Everyone! Not trying to burst your bubble here but it's rarely one thing. More like a shit-ton of things! Now, most of us can't cancel our responsibilities like we can cancel a Fab Fit Fun subscription box. Or move to Mykonos to work at Lindsay Lohan's beach club for funsies. That's not very realistic. But, if I could show you how simply shifting elements of your daily focus can drastically alter and improve how you show up on the daily, would you be in?

Based on your level of stress at the moment, you are either intrigued or you just had an urgent need for a nap. Overwhelm will surely keep you in exhaustion mode. Let me tell you right off the bat that I'm not one to sugarcoat or hit auto-reply. I'm going to give you all the tea, Sis. I'm going to talk to you as a sister, a bestie, an auntie, a wife, a mother, a healer, and a thought leader. I have the self-proclaimed authority to do so because I am all these things. Thank you very much! I hope that you can feel the intention of my words.

If you keep reading, I promise this won't be a cookie cutter approach to leveling up your life and I sure as hell won't advise anything that I haven't done or don't currently practice. I, myself, am a recovering people pleaser, conqueror of chronic anxiety and abandonment issues, autoimmune self-healer, and self-made seven-figure multipreneur. Not to mention that I'm married to the man I fell in love with at fourteen and our five children are happy to call me their heroine. But, on my journey to success, I've had to navigate through some very dark times. Honestly, it took several failures and my mom's diagnosis of early onset dementia to redefine how I see success. I shifted and realigned with my authentic self. I learned to get out of my head and stay grounded in the moment.

Where do you fit into all this? Do you feel unfulfilled no matter how hard you work? Or what you buy? Do you steal extra time from sleep, family, and fun? Do you want more out of life but don't know where to start? Do you see time passing by with zero change? Are you beginning to panic? We're more alike than different, no matter your age, race, religion, or education. I was on that hamster wheel of emotions for years! We may be at various stages in our lives, but the commonality of our existence is that we've been conditioned to see growth through only one lens. We are burnt out from the daily grind, and no matter how much we succeed, we still can't feel fulfillment.

I want to show you a better solution. Even if you take away just one element from this book and apply it to your life, it'll be worth it. One subtle shift can create a ripple effect of positive change in your life. Wayne Dyer said, "If you change the way you look at things, the things you look at change." I am a firm believer in this truth. With this book, I'm using my divine calling to guide you through to embodying the person you are meant to be. It's up to you to do the heavy lifting, though. Will you stay with me as I navigate you through this HOLY SHIFT?

Still here? Good! Now listen up: Being (or becoming) successful isn't about changing who you are. It's about becoming MORE of who you already are. Your authentic self is your True North Star and your secret sauce. The comparison game is brutal and often makes you question your worth. Don't fall into the trap of believing that if you were more like this or that person (someone you admire) that you'd be successful like them. The truth is that your mindset can be the ultimate cock block to your Holy Shift. I want to expose these blocks for you. Here's some more reality: There are people who need you just as you are. Including yourself!

I'm not the Dalai Lama or a doctor of any kind. My calling is my willingness to share my life lessons with you. It's being a messenger of intentional living by sharing my successes and failures with the sincere desire to spare or release you from further inner scrutiny and unnecessary misery. You know. The kind of brutal self-dialogue you wouldn't dare speak of to your friends? Yeah, that kind of insecurity and emotional baggage that no one talks about though we all feel it. You may be reading this in isolation, hungry for change and in need of a motherly guiding hand.

I know you. I see you and, being an empath, I feel you. I know the feeling of emotional pain that makes you question your worth, mortality and your very existence. I want you to know it will be okay and I'll share with you how I turned my pain into my purpose. Now don't be shocked when I give you a nudge, a love punch, or even a kick in the ass. Whatever you need to get from this book is precisely what it will be for you. Only you can decide what you will implement and master or ignore and chalk up to perceived "fluff".

If you are open to acknowledging old patterns that need a shift with a new pair of specs, be prepared to receive a new lens to view your life with. Sometimes, you just need a new prescription to help see things more clearly. To help you refine this newfound vision, this book includes tools that will help you stop and digest the information. Solidify them in your brain and carry them with you for years to come.

The first tool I will give you is a set of questions to ask yourself along the way as you read. Please have a pencil and paper nearby to jot down your answers and flush out the ideas in the margins that come up as you're reading. I encourage you to keep these notes in a progress journal and use them to expand your life focus and track your progress. Trust me, you'll be glad you did when you hit a bump in the road and need inspiration. Seeing all the fabulous progress you've made will boost your self-confidence and give you the steam you'll need to move further along.

The next tool I'll provide you is music. I love hip hop, so I've interspersed some of my favorite hip hop songs for you to ask Alexa to play (or Siri or Cortana). I think you'll find they fit the subjects I'm talking about and may even help solidify the message in your brain. If you don't like hip hop, you don't have to play them, but it would be a good idea to find songs of your own and make a playlist to go along with the chapters and remind you of my message long after you've finished reading.

More tools I'll be adding to your box are gems embedded in the text. Things that have helped me on my journey like Ted Talks, books, quotes, and websites. Be sure to jot down these titles so you can refer to them later.

Last but not least, the greatest tool I'll give you is my story. Everyone knows that a good story contains lessons that carry on for generations to come. I hope that you will find things in my story that relate to your life, and that you will get what you need from my words. I'm speaking to you from my heart and in the same manner in which I speak to my inner circle soul sister squad. So grab your coffee, find your comfy reading spot and let's get into it, Sis.

I often refer to myself as a "Renaissance Gal". It's my clever way of saying I'm peaceful but wild. I need people, yet I want to be alone. I crave adventure but still need quiet. I want spontaneity but, still, I need routine. I love excitement but mostly want calm. Unapologetically, I am needy, wanty, and a giver wrapped into one. I can be all three at the same time, and that doesn't make me weak, wishy-washy, or shy. On the flip side, I'm neither brazen, shameless, nor methodical. I'm multifaceted. It's just how I roll.

The only difference between your perspective and mine is that I now see this dynamic as my superpower rather than my weakness. I no longer perceive my life as chaotic and now deem it as eventful. I now understand how I can make the world fit around my expectations as I create my own version of the American Dream. Once I began to shift my mindset and focus on the important things that are in my control, everything changed. And here's what I know to be true: life is not a balancing act; it's a juggling skill. Master the art of the juggle and your Holy Shift will begin.

Accepting that my life was like a circus was the beginning of my first shift. At home, I have my five children (Bella, Maryn, Beau, Jett & Ardyn), my husband (Mike), and a bearded dragon named Echo. I own and operate three businesses: a dance studio with more than five hundred students and teaching faculty of twenty-three; my team of many leaders in my network marketing business with thousands of promoters; and my personal brand, energy practice, and thousands of customers in between. All are separate entities that need my full attention. Since it's impossible to compartmentalize my life completely, I do compartmentalize responsibilities onto different plates. To give you a sampling of what this is like, I want you to imagine your dining room table with all the different elements of your life on dinner plates. Each plate holds your spouse, children, extended family, friends, work, college, side gig, hobbies, etc. Now pick up each plate, place them on individual fingers and toes and start spinning them just like you'd see on Pier 39 in San Francisco or as a circus act.

Stay with me on this ...

The goal is to have all your responsibilities on plates that are spinning at the same time. How many dishes do you have to pick up? Do you even have enough fingers and toes to spin them on? See, you aren't overwhelmed by accident! You just have a lot of plates and a lot of spinning going on.

I had more spinning plates than fingers and toes, and I knew I had to start dropping some of them. The plates that were too heavy. The ones that were not mine to spin. And the plates that didn't even need my attention. I had a choice. I had to either put on my big girl panties and become the spin master with only the plates that were in highest priority or watch them ALL fall and shatter.

In my twenties, I was a clown. I worked 80+ hours

a week, trying to make everyone happy, struggling to attain the idyllic lifestyle of the perfect mama of two under the age of two, happy wife and playing the peacemaker to my staff while trying to prove myself as a young entrepreneur. I was often sick and repeatedly threw my back out. As a dance instructor, this was a bad situation to keep replaying. In my thirties, as I added another business and more babies, I was introduced to personal development. Books and lectures and training... OH MY! I soon realized that I was in my element; where mindset and empowerment were taught, like-minded relationships & mentorships bonded, new systems developed, and new levels of success were celebrated. I shifted from professional student to impact leader as I implemented the skills I learned to create and replicate a system for my sales team. I evolved in this process and became a successful multipreneur, mom of five, and leader of many.

Now that I've turned forty, I want to share the skills that I have developed and mastered thus far. Thousands of hours and dollars spent on trainings, books, courses and the hard work of implementation of new skills have been vital in my evolution. To be honest, the biggest lesson I learned was to listen for clarity rather than to react. Maybe that's a skill set that only comes with age and emotional maturity, but I now let people process their frustration and don't hastily "clap back" or RSVP to their pity party.

I focus on the result rather than stress over the

work needed to accomplish it, and I remain in pursuit of not giving a shit to pettiness along the way. The latter is a work in progress, and I'll reveal more on this topic later. Being an empath and highly sensitive to people's vibes, I overthink things long enough to spark mini panic attacks, and I create enough self-induced guilt that I could start my own religion.

Once you master the perspective I'm providing in this book, you'll see all your separate plates collectively spinning. Some faster. Some slower. All needing your attention and care. You'll tend to the wobbly plate before it stops and drops while still keeping your focus in macro view. This will keep you sane when you have to go deep on the plates that need your undivided attention. You won't be balancing like you're walking a tightrope. The one foot in front of the other, one wrong move and you fall type of balance. That is like being a one-legged man in an ass kicking contest. You are a human having an experience that isn't paved by a linear path. Just when you get back on track from a trying time in your life, buckle up Sis, you're gonna go off road again soon. This is juggling at its finest and it works for me. Not because I'm special or lucky—it's just a byproduct of honoring how and who I show up for. It's also easier to get back into focus when life knocks you on your ass. I shifted my perception and my workload once I decided which plates were of the highest priority and kept those plates in motion. Simple and efficient yet so hard to do when your ego is screaming at you to do more, be more, have more, and consume more.

Yeah, circus and plates metaphor may be juvenile. I've taught children for over 25 years, so it's in my nature to break things down into more realistic concepts. I keep the lesson simplistic but now, comes your first love punch: your life is YOUR circus. Those are YOUR monkeys. No one is coming to save you or spin the plates for you. So you can either keep clown'n around, trying to spin them all. Or you can SHIFT and start auditing which plates to pick up, which ones to drop and work the remaining plates like a Ringmaster.

I want to help you master your plate spinning and shift that hustle into a state of flow. This book contains new ways to look at your daily life and teaches you how to acknowledge old wounds that have kept you from creating a life by design. Once you begin to implement this juggling act, you will be your own catalyst of your Holy Shift!

*It's disrespectful to yourself
to not have downtime.*

-Lindsey

HUSTLE < FLOW

I used to glorify the grind. I was a self-proclaimed hustler and bragged about busting my ass on the daily. Looking back, I thought it was the only way to get respect. When social media became the new normal, I was able to check in online and verbally vomit my daily routine. Holding my protein shake in my perfectly positioned selfie made it all too easy to scale my audience. I was hooked. I rocked the hustle: checking into the gym, often twice a day, posting myself on calls, always flossing that busy life, my kids and their blog worthy birthday decor and let's take a moment of silence for all rants regarding the school parking lot. I liked to vaguebook with cliffhanger posts, which we all know is posting vague but intriguing sentences to get the "what's wrong?" in the comment section. I was a savage!

When my memories posts pop up on Facebook and I see my keyboard cowboy behavior, I literally shake my damn head. In my defense, it was 2006, and social media was basically like my public diary and my outlet for the severe anxiety in my life. I was trying to balance and failing miserably yet found peace in letting my life play out online. I fell into the trap of thinking that, in order to be successful, I had to tell myself and anyone who would listen, that success wasn't for the emotionally weak or for those who didn't strive to be an overachiever.

Looking back, I was force feeding this mindset to other women who had no desire to hustle like that. In my relentless pursuit of grandeur boss babe euphoria, I realized that hustling wasn't even in alignment with my core beliefs. I now realize I wasted precious time playing out hypothetical stories in my head and having a pissing contest with people. No joke, everyone was fair game. Like, if we were next to one another on the treadmill at the gym. Guess what, pal? We were now racing on these treadmills. That was my level of competitiveness. In hindsight, I alienated myself from friends and family. Even though family and connection are my core values, I was doing the very things that would cause a divide. It was the world vs. me. Yeah, I was crazy pants. Social media can create this voyeur soapbox behavior. I felt like I was on my own reality show. Like I was being watched at every turn, and I had to be an example of excellence. Now, an example to whom? Excellence of what? Everyone and everything! I was literally on a loop of needing to prove my worth and also exemplify all things fabulous when, truth be told, I was a ticking time bomb.

I'll save you the trouble and tell you right now: hustling will get you no further than the treadmill you are on. It will keep you moving, but it won't take you anywhere. You'll get tired, and you'll get off for a breather, then realize you're behind and get right back on the mill for a big ole burnout. Don't do what I did in my early years. Save yourself and get off the tread-mill for good.

Your path should be paved with intentional living. Also known as living life on purpose. We'll talk about this more as we go along, but for now, know that you don't have to hustle and you don't have to be the best at everything you try. Your aim should be to flow or move along steadily towards your goal, learning along the way.

As you begin to shift from hustle to flow, you will often doubt yourself or experience FOMO. Fear of missing out is the social media-induced paranoia caused by seeing what everyone else is doing and comparing yourself to them. Everyone is #doingit-forthegram and one-upping everyone else, so the stan-dard is set ridiculously high. What you may not realize is that people only post their happiest moments or the highlights of their life. Don't be fooled by all the filters and smiles! You must abort all FOMO behavior immediately. I don't mean close all your accounts, but maybe set a timer for social media and most definitely unfollow the accounts that make you feel insecure about yourself. If you have to delete apps from your phone to be more productive, then do it! Setting boundaries to the rabbit hole effect that social media creates with endless scrolling is a sure fire way to shift focus toward what you need to be doing. Unless you'd rather be watching what everyone is eating for lunch or wearing to the gym?

Once you free yourself from these time wasters, you'll find it easier to be in a state of flow. Remember that flow will inspire you to release excess shit that keeps you overwhelmed. FOMO causes anxiety which triggers your basic instinct to revert to old patterns and add more plates to spin. Less is the new more, Sis! Not having your apps readily available to access will make a huge impact on your constant need to refresh your feed throughout the day. It's important to note that one reason we stay busy is to keep us from feeling and healing. In the same manner that picking at a scab only to reopen a wound, this too happens to us emotionally if we fail to address our rooted pain points. One small "pick" at our life and we lose our shit. Why do we do this? Well, sitting with your emotions and doing a self-audit is super uncomfortable and who wants to sit with those kinds of feelings? So, we don't. Instead, we fill the pain with our numbing method of choice: alcohol, pills, food, buying stuff, staying busy. Then we remain in overwhelm to keep us distracted and go about our lives in this same loop.

Love punch question: so how's that been working for ya?

I used to hustle hard believing all the biz one-liners like "success isn't a sprint; it's a marathon." It was my friend and mentor, Nick Sarnicola, who told me that life is actually a marathon of sprint races. Short bursts, with ebbs and flows where you learn to rest but not quit. The hustle and grind or the start then stop will burn you out quick. Alexa, play "Pop, Lock and Drop It," by Huey.

Being in a state of flow will keep you consistent and also more adept to thinking under pressure. I didn't comprehend how to do "flow" until my late thirties. Before that, I wore my grind as a badge of honor. I was legit proud that I was SO busy all the time as if my identity was built on multitasking in a constant state of overwhelm. Like, wasn't this how all successful people lived their life? I was convinced this was the right path. I was a cluster; paranoid, defensive, and angry. I was always in a hurry, had zero patience, and anxiety attacks galore. See, binging on coffee and navigating daily life in fight or flight mode will make you a lil cray. I was in a self-induced volatile emotional space, always feeling victimized and exhausted. Now add big goals, a bunch of babies, a competitive dance business (with some crazy dance moms), the drama that transpired could have been scripted for television. I had the complete framework for a total shit show with an all-star supporting cast.

Where's my star on the Hollywood Walk of Fame? I'll wait.

Being busy all the time is not in your best interest. Neither is the constant need to feel in competition with everyone else. It's disrespectful to yourself to not have downtime. I ask you to reflect on how you feel when you take a day to veg out. I'll bet you get a rush of guilt, with some underlying anxiety splashed with shame and a big ole "shoulda" as the cherry on top. With this *I should be doing this* or *I could have done that* type of nonsense self-talk, you are shoulding all over yourself. Cue the self-sabotaging loop.

Release the need to hustle to be successful. Shift your gears to an intentional flow. We are human BEINGS, not human DOINGS. Here's the thing— people that sprint without taking any breaks are living under the illusion that, one day, life is just naturally going to slow down. Anyone who has taken a second to think that line of thought all the way through knows that's just not how it works. Even worse are the chest banging egomaniacs telling you how hard they work and how amazing they are. I'll tell you this. In business, I've been to the peek of my own "mountain top" on several occasions. The air is fresher to breathe, and the climb and building of momentum to the peak is exhilarating... for a brief moment. What no one tells you is that once you reach the pinnacle, you become the standard. Once the standard, you now become the target. And therein lies the rub. Once you get to the top, it's an even harder fight to stay there. Alexa, play "Diva" by Beyonce.

Time won't slow down for you to catch up. You have just become so focused on hustling all those plates that before long either you or a plate breaks. Controlling the pace in which you spin your plates can positively change your life experience. Not only for you but for your loved ones. The hustle pace can be used seasonally but only if taking into consideration what season of life you are in. I'm speaking as a mother to a mother with a calling here. You must savor your season, Sis. Having little ones at home and trying to stay in hustle will only keep you pissed off and resentful. If you are frustrated because you can't do what you want to do when you want to do it, you will stay bitter toward your kids. Later, you'll regret the quality time you missed out on when they are grown. This cycle is real and vicious. It's time to open your eyes and acknowledge what season you are in and just be there, in that moment with zero guilt.

Now for those who are entering their season of flow, you are best served to get the buy-in of your spouse and family to ensure your support. Being on the same page where the fam knows what to expect will play a huge role in your ability to flow. Want to know what else plays a huge role in your success? By paying attention to who motivates you.

Mama, this is heavy on my heart... If you follow, admire and/or want to emulate other boss babes online who have zero children or a family dynamic that is different from yours, know it can be a surefire way to burn out when times get tough. I recommend that you seek inspiration from those who've created a lifestyle that you want to live. Seek those who resemble the family dynamic you want or have already but at a level you aspire to be at. Your season of growth is here. It's time to flow. So set your intentions and ask for help to keep you sane; knowing that your desire to hustle is your preference rather than an obligation. Just be careful to have realistic mentors that you deem the standard for success.

Another lesson I have learned about hustling is that you can't outrun stress. I was comfortably running 25 miles a week, and the fear was still there. You can't ignore anxiety and you sure as hell can't quit your mission. Something has to give so you can stay in the flow. My "Aha" moment was realizing that stress is genuinely there to teach me that something needed healing. When my anxiety was there it was because I felt that I wasn't supported and valued and I didn't do anything to change it. Heaven forbid I ask for help. My chronic anxiety, abandonment issues, and not speaking my truth were hindering my healing and blocking my blessings.

A few years ago, I woke up. I realized that how I've chosen to deal with stress and also how I ran my businesses needed a major shift. Aligning with how I wanted to feel and what I wanted to experience in my daily life was not giving me peace. So I pivoted. HARD. I stepped into my power, found my voice and started handing off plates that I no longer wanted to spin. I didn't know what impact those changes would have on my livelihood, but I knew they no longer sparked joy. So I Marie Kondo'd TF out of my businesses. Shifting resulted in the most significant release of stress. I experienced an inner peace, unlike anything I've ever felt before.

Look, Sis, if you're experiencing a higher than usual amount of mental or emotional tension in your life, business, or both, take this opportunity to reassess. Throughout this book, I share the many shifts I made to create a more peaceful mindset which naturally gives you a higher quality of life. Notice that I said nothing about money. Money follows. It should never lead. Your focus should be on what's working and what's not working. What feels aligned and what feels not aligned? Once you identify the things that are no longer working or aligned, be courageous enough to let them go. Even if you don't know what to do next … Let it go. Don't follow the trend and glorify being busy or being PRODUCTive. You'll just end up throwing yourself deeply into entrapment. Productive means you are a product of labor. You betta recognize! Alexa, play "Check Yo Self" by Ice Cube.

Making a pivot in my business meant I gave away a significant income for free. I wrapped it in a bow and handed it over. It turns out, my stress and anxiety weren't worth the revenue. Personally, I do not know of anyone who has done this without trying to get a piece of that pie. For me, no strings attached is best and wouldn't you know it, I was able to double the income I gave away by simply aligning with other things that lit a fire in my soul. I trusted the universe. I risked earning less income in order to close this anxiety loop rather than repeat it and remain the same. You cannot put a price tag on inner peace, Sis. Alexa, play "Julia" by ZSA.

I want you to seek what excites you and go all in. Flow can only happen when you stop fighting yourself, and this can only occur when you begin to take steps that mesh with who you are and what you want to do in this life. But, what if it hurts to let go of old wounds and acknowledge what bothers you? Welp, you'll have to feel some pain. Oh, this essential sensory guide that hurts like a motherfucker. I know transformation can be painful but trust that you're not falling apart. You're falling into something beautiful. Pain will break you down to nothing, like a crucible. But just as the Phoenix rises from ashes, you become reborn. Renewed. Rejuvenated.

As we rise in love collectively, we heal. You are rising above your shadow knowing that pain does not seek to destroy you. Pain comes in waves of healing love. Just as you labor in birth, your pain is the labor towards your breakthrough. So sit with the pain. Do not seek to fight it. You are treading the water, just don't drown in it. Invite it in, let the tears flow until you simply cannot cry anymore. Stay in your heart space and allow the feelings to pass through, carrying emotional pain as well as physical. What a privilege it is to be gifted with this life. You're climbing a mountain, Sis. This pain is your pathway to peace. Breathe in love. Breathe out resistance and the thought that pain will destroy you. Pain will liberate you if you choose to allow the transformation.

Healers are often the ones who have become so comfortable with the pain that they have chosen to learn from it and use it as a stepping stone to all things divine. We don't allow our pain or the pain of the world to make us suffer unknowingly; we choose to transmute it into something beautiful. One of my favorite ways to shift the hustle to the flow is to get out in nature. Now, I'm not going to lie—I'm a glamping gal so I don't necessarily mean you have to be sleeping in a tent or roughing it to get in touch with nature. That said, nature is a healer. Period. When we allow ourselves to really feel by clearing our mind, putting our bare feet to the earth, let go the chatter in our head, feel the pain we feel and ugly cry, we release this energy and free up our inner real estate.

A dear friend and integrated energy healer taught me this: trees inhale carbon dioxide and exhale oxygen, while we inhale oxygen and exhale carbon dioxide. So, when we release and exhale the heaviness inside of us, Mother Nature inhales it as life, as food, as nourishment, and then exhales, giving us back what we need most: healing. It is a perfect cycle. What we release, she takes in; and what she releases, we take in. We have so much support when we choose to see it's there for us in nature.

11

What if you are in extreme hustler mode (it's a thing) and you are waiting for the perfect time to enjoy your life? Well, I hate to break it to you, but people wait their whole lives for the "right time" to do things, and then they die with regret. So, just do the damn thing!!! Drink your best champagne whenever you want. Serve Taco Tuesday on your fancy dinnerware. Smoke the Cuban cigar that you've been saving for a special occasion on a random Sunday afternoon. Wear heels even though you have casual dinner plans. Enjoy more sunsets. Take more trips. Create more moments. Here's the secret—we aren't promised tomorrow. Being alive is a special occasion!!

Getting in our own corner is nearly step one of many in making the necessary changes we want to make. I like to stay affirmed AF in the process. Affirmations go a long way in calming the mind and body down and refocusing on something positive. When you are busy but you know the universe has got you in flow life feels so much better. Today's affirmation goes like this: thick thighs saves lives, call me little buttercup." Yes, my random daily affirmations are lyrics from Lizzo, most days from Cardi B., and I'm pretty sure I affirmed myself to Ariana Grande yesterday. Do what works for you, boo.

On a serious note, here are my exact daily affirmations for anxiety:

> *I trust the universe 1000%.*
> *I evoke my soul self to the surface.*

I now let self love in.
I am fully protected by the universe.
It's okay to love myself unconditionally.
I am ready to let go of conditions.
Anxiety, I hear you.
I now let self love in.
Now fill in the blank: I am grateful
    for_____.

Speak abundance in absolutes and abundance will flow to you. This practice is not "woo woo" shiz. Abundance is a mindset, and when you focus on what you want, all the while being grateful for what you have, you are winning. I believe the universe 1000% has my back. Do you??

You have to get clear on what you really desire, and if you're unsure ask yourself these questions:

What do you:

- Crave?
- Desire more of?
- Wish for?
- Dream about?
- What do you want more than anything?

WRITE your answers down in Holy Shift! Worksheet #1. I promise you this: Once you can answer these questions and find your truths, you are on your next level of enlightenment. You'll be in your flow.

Because when you are specific about what the fuck you want, the universe will align for you.

In my early twenties, I felt that everything negative in my life was happening to me. It wasn't until I was thirty years old when I realized life was happening for me. I felt a newfound stability in my emotions and less in defensive. The real breakthrough came when my mother didn't call me on my birthday. I was thirty-five and the reality of her declining mental health was like a kick to my gut. Shortly thereafter, I hit my rock bottom. I simply could not take the heartache anymore. So, I decided to surrender. I began to dive deep into my Reiki practice and spent the next 5 years working with April, my integrated energy healer & mentor. Reiki practice helped me shift to see this painful experience with my mom as happening THROUGH me. That's when I began to align with flow.

Hustle is the resistance and the fight. Flow is allowance and acceptance. Flow is not passive. Don't get it twisted. It's highly active. The truth is we live in an abundant world. I believe I have an abundant life even though I have to navigate through the pain points. Now, that's not to say that there isn't a real struggle and hurting people who have genuinely fallen on hard times. But the truth remains that there is enough for us all. The only thing keeping you from abundance is your belief that you deserve it and your willingness to surrender to the pain. Alexa, play "Still Brazy" by YG.

If you don't agree, that's your perception. Let me explain. All that remains is for you to choose whether you'll be abundance focused (flow) or consumed by the feeling of impossible or lack (hustle). The moment you become non-negotiable about changing your mental zip code, pack your bags and mentally move to a new zip code filled with prosperity instead of scarcity, you will begin to see your life change. It's not geography, it's psychology. The moment you begin to think as prosperous people think, study what prosperous people study and be more intentional about attracting what you want to attract, your life will start to flow. The moment you shift your mindset is the moment that your finances, relationships, and physical wellness will follow. Holy Shift!

I'm your sister in prosperity and possibility, but you have to do this for you. You have to see past your current situation and do something NOW. I'm rooting for all of us to be woke AF and flow'n. Acknowledge that your inner critic is a terrified naysayer and you wouldn't trust a terrified naysayer to cut your bangs. Yet you continue to let your inner critic keep you small. Unsubscribe from Ms. Paralyzed With Fears' opinion. Quiet the mind and train it to see abundance. See, your mind is like a puppy. You have to train it, or it shits everywhere.

When I am loving myself unconditionally, I allow others to be where they are. I stop trying to be the fixer for them and just let them be. Being with someone who loves you precisely for who you are and doesn't want to change you or fix you is the most refreshing experience. Obviously not in an "I'll tolerate who you are because it's the right thing to do" type of love, But, being with someone who genuinely adores all of the parts of you and doesn't see anything that needs fixing. We all deserve love like that. The feeling of being in love is merely being in alignment with your true self.

Many people only allow themselves to experience this feeling when someone else focuses on loving them. The truth is that we have the ability to allow this feeling all the time. When we open the doors to loving ourselves without judgment, the dam breaks open to flow. It's challenging to fight with life when you unconditionally love yourself. But, how do you learn to have unconditional love for yourself when you are loved conditionally? It all starts from within. I want to permit you to align with your true Self. Alexa, play "Far Alone" by G-Eazy.

What do you:

- Crave?

- Desire more of?

- Wish for?

- Dream about?

....

....

....

- What do you want more than anything?

....

....

....

Being bold is your birthright.

-Lindsey

PERMISSION TO ALIGN

When we align, we thrive! What does it mean to align or be in alignment? Technically, it means to be in a straight line or agreement. Personal alignment means to be in line or agreement with who you are, how you feel, and what you do in your life. If you are a creative free spirit but feel trapped at a job that you dread, you're not in alignment. I know this may seem ~ious when you read it. However, sometimes, when ~f alignment, we justify our position into ⌐out it.

ese questions (write ⌐eet #2 if you are a

1. What do you love to spend your time doing?
2. Who do you love to spend your time with?
3. What are you good at?
4. What problem, if any, would you feel passionate about solving?
5. What does the world need?

In the center of our answers to the above questions, we find our purpose — It's the sweet spot. We don't have to change to achieve our purpose. We merely need to remember who we are and become more of that. This is also called being our authentic selves. Believe it or not, we might be hiding some of this from ourselves because we are afraid of judgment, persecution, or even our safety. We need to find a safe place where we can explore who we are and overcome the programming in our head that tells us who we can't be.

Being authentic, or in alignment, with ourselves means finding hidden traits, wants, needs, and desires that we've kept bottled up for years. We don't need to keep ourselves hidden any longer. What may have kept us safe ten years ago is suffocating us now, and it's time to open up our internal closet and see what's in there. You'll need to ask more questions than I have listed above, but at least these will get you started. Give yourself permission to align with yourself now; don't wait until you think there will be a better place to stop and do this. Now is the right time.

I permitted myself to align when my mom was diagnosed. I was thirty-three, and suddenly scared shitless of my own mortality. I immediately gave myself permission to live my life unapologetically. It was an instantaneous shift for me but what angers me the most is that it took my mother's diagnosis of an incurable disease to spark a mindset that I should have been embodying all along. My mother, Marilyn, a beautiful, bright light to everyone on the outside but dreadfully insecure and paranoid on the inside. She was so elegant and gracious but never really saw how others saw her, and as a result, she always felt insecure. Like mother, like daughter, I often found myself in this self-deprecating loop.

Now that my mother is sixty-four and in full-time care facility, she isn't concerned with what others think of her. She doesn't ask about her husband, her grandkids, her friends, the latest news. She used to never leave the house without a full face of makeup, and now she never wears it. Seeing my mom's shift, was my wake up call to embody who I am, what I stand for and how I show up in the world. I have been insecure about so many things: my top heavy body type, having to wear glasses since I was five, and my large forehead; to name a few. I vowed to stop spending time picking myself apart, wishing I was different, and start loving myself as I am.

Years of self-scrutiny and social anxiety as a child doesn't disappear as an adult. It only expands. So much so, that I would walk by a group of strangers and pray they wouldn't notice me for they might find some reason to judge me. I would hear laughter and immediately assume they were laughing at me. Now I am a fearless performer as a dancer. But, take me out of my comfort zone, and I am an introverted, shy person. You may believe you need a nose or boob job, or to lose weight to gain the confidence you lack. I'm here to tell you that you can completely change your body, and get the surgery, botox, and fillers. But unless you quiet that inner critic, get to the root cause of your pain and begin your path toward healing you will never embody true confidence. I've spent years healing and working on reprogramming my brain to change how I see myself.

My shift in calming my inner critic began when I started to see myself through the eyes of my children. Their unconditional love was the quickest way to find my peace of mind. They love me as I am: thicker, smaller, dressed up or looking a hot mess. I am worthy of love just the way I am. So why am I withholding my self-love when I'm not satisfied with my looks? It's a personal betrayal to put ourselves through this and for what? Does self-loathing feel good? Absolutely not. Yet, we continue to compare ourselves to people who look perfectly polished on our Insta feed. We covet everyone else but ourselves and wonder why we are so insecure. My mom suffered from lack of self-love, I then followed her lead. So, I want to show you how to make this shift of self-shaming to self-acceptance.

I miss and physically ache for my mom. She's still

alive and I can see her every day, but that's not the same person. That is the shell of the fiery woman who raised me. She can only be in the moment she's in and some distant memories she's memorized from retelling the same stories. I wish my mom would have loved herself and experienced this new found freedom of alignment with me. However, I owe my shift to her. Had she been everything I ever needed and wanted as a mother, I wouldn't have embarked on my journey at all. I am determined to do it for both of us, healing this generational curse. I am creating a renaissance within because unless I change, nothing changes. If the cycle remains, no one wins. It literally stops with me.

Knowing who you are and only saying yes to people, experiences, and careers that align with you is a daily conscious process. Emotional growth can look like this:

- You'll make mistakes on the way to your vision.

  Identify and correct them.

- You'll lose folks on the path to your vision.

  Mourn and replace them.

- You'll face challenges on the path to your vision.

Assess and oust them.

Your greatest asset will be your ability to adjust without losing alignment.

Being bold is your birthright. It's not only safe to be yourself; it's necessary.

Part of the key elements to alignment is realizing the distinction between the following driving forces in your life:

1. A Job
2. A Career
3. A Calling

I beg you to stop doing what you think others want of you in your job and career. Allow yourself to discover your calling. Imagine taking back all of the energy you have ever spent trying to explain yourself to people. Letting go of the need to explain yourself to others is freedom. How many times has your mind been trying to throw self-doubt at you? Telling you someone doesn't understand you, is judging you, or doesn't respect you? Then you speak with the person and realize you made the whole scenario up in your head.

Even if your fears were justified, why do you give them so much weight? It's because, since infancy, we have been socially conditioned to be "likable" as a way to ensure our needs are met by our parents and other loved ones. So we become disproportionately focused on trying to control what others think of us. The moment when you realize you're the only one whose judgments of you actually have a real impact on your life is the moment you shift. Alexa, play "Live Your Life" by T.I.

As we ponder our life's purpose or calling, it is critical to know that we can dream big.

I want to be completely honest here. I did not have elephant-dick-sized goals as a kid. I wanted to do everything that I thought was cool. I also wanted to have a lot of babies with little thought of who my husband would be. Joey from New Kids On The Block was my second choice. My first crush was Patrick Swayze. He was a handsome dancer, wore black, and wouldn't let Baby sit in the corner. Where do I sign the marriage certificate?! As for my career choice? I recall wanting to be a judge when I was nine. I loved being in charge, but my insecurity kicked in. I bullied myself out of this future career when I found myself perplexed over how I would decide who goes to jail. Heck, I couldn't decide what my favorite color was. This career choice was too black and white for me. I'm more of a rainbow kinda gal, so I switched my sights to being a veterinarian.

My hopes of saving animals quickly dissolved when my mother brought to my attention that only sick animals are brought to the vet. My mom wasn't being a dream crusher, she just knew I had a tender heart for animals. She had endured many car rides with me sobbing in my booster seat, hands to face and in disbelief after I saw a dead animal on the side of the road. In 6th grade, I started babysitting for income. I read *The Baby Sitters Club* series and watched the movie *Adventures in Babysitting*. Clearly, I was perfect for the gig. I made my own business cards. I cut them out from pastel blue construction paper. I even wrote my name and phone number on them in my best handwriting. I made money watching kiddos on the weekends and, at fourteen, I landed my first job as a receptionist for a local small business. I have always been very independent and loved earning my own money. However, I didn't really know what I wanted to do for my career.

It's hard for people to even think about possibilities and dreams when they can only see themselves inside their current situation. Dreams seem impossible when you are in survival mode. At seventeen, I was in survival mode. In fact, my senior year in high school is a blur but I'll get into this later. My dream of being a dance studio owner was less planned out and more of an opportunity that just presented itself. I was seventeen and our local studio owner announced her retirement.

I knew that if I didn't take the chance and open a spot, someone else would. So, I asked for a loan from my mom and found a location to lease. I took my plan to my dad to get my floor built and we just launched it. The only business skills I had were from handwriting my babysitting cards. But, once I made a decision, all that I needed came into my life so effortlessly.

This is how alignment works. I saw an opportunity, I acted, and twenty-three years later, I'm still in love with what I have created.

So I want to help you find some alignment in your calling. Even if you are still trying to figure out what it really is. The easiest way for me to help you is by reverse engineering your dreams. I want you to make a list of the things you DON'T want or that no longer work for your life. Expanding on that list, add what needs to happen to not be in survival mode.

Example:

- I do not want to struggle to pay my rent.

  Goal: an income source that allows me to not only rent but have money left over to invest.

- I do not want to yell at my kids.

  Goal: I will stop, take a deep breathe and count to 10 before I react or raise my voice.

These steps may seem elementary but when you get your head above your current financial state or emotional triggers, you will see this process helps tremendously. You can develop your dream list, but until you are specific in what you want, you'll kinda sorta get results.

Dreaming big is unique to the dreamer. If you are reading this and thinking that you are a successful stay at home mom and that is your dream role, then embody it, mama! Being the CEO of your home is something to be proud of. The WORST thing you can ever do is feel shamed by other people's shoulds. "You should be a _____ not a _____" is not in your highest good, Sis. You are the only person that has the right to decide because you know yourself best. When I was young, I didn't know what I wanted to do as an adult but I knew I wanted to teach and loved to help people. I realized quickly that I didn't want a 9-5 workday. Or to have a boss. So, I became an entrepreneur that allowed me to be home with my littles during the day and work at night.

Another fact you need to come to terms with is that money doesn't equal happiness. I know multi-millionaires who are lonely and also have friends who work blue collar jobs and are very happy with their lives. Money is fun and fundamentally necessary if you want to do big things. I love expensive shit so I want to make money to afford those things. However, that doesn't make me greedy. I head to the discounted rack first when I go to a store and love a good sale. It makes me self aware and practical according to my personal goals. Frankly, there are days when I felt that my dreams were too big. My soul whispered to my ego, "Slow your roll, Bish. Can't you just chill and be content with what you have?" I knew I wanted a large family and I knew I wanted to be an entrepreneur. So

I ran with that, learning when to sprint and when to walk. Regardless of how fast I went, I never stopped the movement toward my goals.

Let's talk about that movement for a moment. Remember when you were in the bathtub as a little girl, and you pushed your body with your toes until you bumped the other end with your head, and then you relaxed your toes and went back to the other end? You were making big waves in the water and enjoying the fruits of your movement. When you stopped moving the waves would get smaller and smaller, and you'd hold as still as you could until the water was calm again.

The same thing happens to the people and things around us when we are moving and shaking things up, and also when we slow down or stop altogether. When we stop moving and plant ourselves in front of the tv, we lose our motivation and our friends and family will follow suit, calling us less often and talking less about the dreams we once told them about. When we are moving toward our goals, we are happier because we always have a taste of our dreams within reach and we are still in touch with ourselves and what we want. The absence of movement can cause depression and doubt. We don't have anything to look forward to anymore, and we don't have any momentum to propel us forward.

The good news is that we can create movement whenever we want. Even if it's a small change at first. Movement is movement.

Move toward your fulfillment whilst embodying your gifts. If I asked you what those gifts are, what would you say? What are you good at? What gives you joy? My purpose is to impact others and teach them to be unapologetic about who they are. I love to find out what makes people tick and how they rock 'n' roll. I want to be the spark for you but something tells me that you need a love punch. My love punch for you: stop waiting for the stars to align or your horoscope to tell you that by not deciding to take the first step, you're deciding to do nothing. Your gifts have been with you this whole time. You just haven't downloaded them yet. Now it's time to unleash who've you've always been. She's ready.

Take a moment to think about your favorite things, your favorite subjects in school, and the things you are drawn to in life. What do you find yourself doing that you have a hard time taking yourself away from? Maybe you are an artist, and you need to develop your talent or discover different mediums. Or you are a saleswoman, and it shows in the way you are always getting your friends to try the products you believe in and know will work for them, too. Perhaps you are a budding professor? You are a perpetual learner and you don't ever want to leave the school atmosphere. Write this all down and explore the possibilities of what your gifts might bring: if I do x, then what happens to y? Sometimes it helps to get ideas from others, so get together with a group of friends and ask them some of these same questions. Their answers might produce a spark for you.

One of my strengths is that I'm an early adopter. I love new ways, new concepts, and forward thinking. I also love to learn new things which has shifted my belief about losing. I never lose. I only learn. I'm a learner, willing to chance failures to grow from my experiences. Now this is mortifying to my husband. He would rather know in absolutes before treading into the unknown waters. I think that our yin yang personality types help to keep a balance. You too can be a pioneering, early adopter. You see, your fear of failure keeps you from even trying. You don't learn the best lessons from your achievements but from your failures along the way.

Giving you permission to align is basically my way of asking you to step up and try. Some try for a few months and if it doesn't make them an instant success, they quit and find fault in surrounding elements to let themselves off the proverbial hook. Let me make this perfectly clear: some people are out to see you fail due to their own insecurities. Deep down they are glad you quit. They are glad you stayed small and gave up because, now, they don't have to compare themselves to you. It's awful but it's reality. This is when my stubbornness is my asset. Those types of people in my life only fuel my fire. Successful people are not afraid to fail because they take calculated risks. No risk. No reward.

Let's not forget that it's never too late to be who

you secretly want to become. Finding ourselves can be difficult. It feels like a constant battle between who we think we are and who we actually are. The world tells us one thing, while our inner being and intuition says another. The louder the world's opinion, the more drowned out our inner voice becomes. Finding our truth and our purpose may feel like a constant battle because we have been taught not to trust ourselves and not to rely on the power and strength that is within. Returning to who we are may take time, but it's a journey that we must make for ourselves and by ourselves. Your ability to reach your goals is more about the inner transformation and becoming the person you are meant to be and less about the actual goal itself.

I think we sometimes get caught up in other people's lives and dreams. We believe that their dreams are our dreams too. Or that the life they live is the life we want to live. Sometimes, we even mirror our success with others' success. Or we mirror ourselves in a reflection of somebody else's image. If we were to mute the constant distractions, looking too often to the left or right rather than focusing forward on our own path, I don't really think we would want to be anyone else that much, or even have the same dreams and goals as they do.

Sometimes, we have our own dreams, but the world is so loud we can't hear them. We forget to listen because of all the chaos. Frankly, it's easier to focus on how far ahead everyone else seems to be.

The noise of the external world is muting the sound of the internal world. Our intuition pays the price.

Last night, I went to bed feeling a bit moody because, unfortunately, I had a moment of comparison. I compared myself to something which has never even been a dream of mine. But it looked appealing. I sat with myself in silence afterward and promised myself always to remember why I do what I do, and that I am exactly where I need to be. Life has its way of pulling us back towards ourselves constantly, through lessons, pain, and growth.

We need to be no one else but ourselves. Our path has been carved uniquely with our purpose. You might not like hearing that if you are a rebel like me and want to create your own path. Don't worry. You still get to do that. Your path is yours, and no one else's. You're not destined to be something you despise. On the contrary, your path is filled with things you will love, crave and strive for. You are blind to your path, though. We are all born blind and we must feel our way through the darkness until we can truly see our calling.

You have all the wisdom and guidance that you need within you. You just have to recognize that it is there. Look within. Find your authentic self. But you don't have to do this alone. As you go along this path called alignment, take notice of the people who are right next to you. They may be at a different pace or on a different path, but they are right there with you experiencing similar pains, successes, and mile markers. They probably have picked up a few things that could be useful to you. Say hi!

You need a running buddy in life and entrepreneurship. I'm so fortunate to have a few great ladies along for the ride. If you don't have one, I'll be her! When you align, you flow, and that's when you bloom —even with obstacles in your path. I have genuinely embodied a goal that I set years ago to be in alignment, develop, and grow myself as a person and help others to do the same. I want to lead with intention rather than calculation, and I want to let intention be the catalyst in all that I do. I want to master the art of fulfillment by collecting moments and being present. I know you want this as well. Let's line it up, ladies! Alexa, play "Formation" by Beyonce.

- What do you love to spend your time doing?

_____

_____

_____

- Who do you love to spend your time with?

_____

_____

_____

- What are you good at?

_____

_____

_____

- What problem, if any, would you feel passionate about solving?

_____

_____

_____

- What does the world need?

_____

_____

_____

*The blessed don't beef with the
miserable.*

-Lindsey

3

KNOW WHO THE FUCK YOU ARE

Polonius gave some profound advice to his son Laertes when he was embarking for France. He said, "To thy own self be true." My version is "Know who the fuck who you are!" You must give yourself the opportunity to get this part straight because you are the foundation of what you build the rest of your life on. If you aren't clear on this, it can get very confusing and, for many, even depressing.

I'm a teacher by trade, creative by heart, and a leader on purpose. It doesn't matter to me where others stand because I know where I stand and who I stand for. My life is a balance between what I can and can't control. I'm learning to live between effort and surrender and I hope that my pursuit of a life less ordinary will inspire others to do the same. I truly believe that, in some way, that's what we all desire: knowing who we are, accepting that person, and doing something helpful in this world.

There are some roadblocks that seem to get in our way. Let's start with this gem: get out of your head. Sounds easy, but you'd be shocked if you made a conscious effort to tally how many mean thoughts trolled between your ears each day. Your perspective can either be your power or your prison. If you think it's hard to create good habits, don't dwell on that fact. It takes practice, so start now by getting out of your head and following your gut. Seek your truth to gain the greatest advantage you'll ever have in life. The only way to get to your truth is through experience. They weren't lying when they told you:

Your test will be your testimony.

Your mess will be your message.

The problem many people face is that think they shouldn't have any problems. So, the real formula for influencing others is going through massive pain, failure, turmoil, and struggle. Then pulling through to tell your story. People don't care to see you living your best life as much as they love to learn about your growth, lessons, and the discipline you developed along the way. This is your impact.

I gag at the word "influencer" because I believe we are all influential. If you got your toddler to stop that tantrum in the grocery aisle, SIS, you are indeed an influencer! Those who can show you their pits along with their peaks so you can navigate the mountain better are truly the iconic ones. So, go share the lesson. Share your story even if your voice cracks. You'll be stronger because you'll be stepping into your truth and, ultimately, freeing yourself in the process. What you hide owns you. So be free and impact others along the way. Speak your truth even if you know it's not what they want to hear. Honoring your voice is mandatory!

My husband, Mike, usually cringes when I speak my feelings to a store manager or in public. But if I don't, I literally feel my neck begin to ache. Sorry. Not sorry, babe. My body is responding. Therefore, I need to act on it. Today, I choose my words and speak from how I'm feeling rather than absolute. Shifting my dialogue from 'You always hurt my feelings when you never say you are sorry' to 'Not acknowledging that my feelings are hurt regardless of your intentions is why I'm upset' has opened up more dialogue and brought more closure when having an argument with Mike. This has made all the difference. It keeps me open to sharing how I received him instead of accusing or labeling. Understand that we are all working through past trauma, anger, ego, and over-whelm. I no longer have a need to blame. I have a need to express rather than repress.

Speaking my truth rather than suppressing it transformed the golf ball sized goiter in my neck to no lump at all. The Hashimoto's diagnosis in 2012 to no longer testing for the disease. I'm telling you, what you silence will make you sick. What you hide holds you hostage. So, if I feel something is unjust or I need to speak up, I do it.

It's all part of knowing yourself, where your

boundaries lie, and what you need to do to stay healthy. How you feel about yourself affects everything else. It sets the tone for all of your relationships. If you love and respect yourself, you will love and respect others. If you loathe yourself, you will loathe others. In relationships, you'll get what you put out there mirrored back to you. Therefore you must set expectations and be an example of what you want, need, and expect. If you coast through, kinda sorta giving clues of what you want, you will in return get a kinda-sorta relationship. Self-love is sacred, Sis! If you want something different, go within first, then out. My job is to make peace with myself over and over and over again until I'm the stillest, clearest channel for the spirit to exist within.

My goal is to be so completely myself that everyone around me is safe to be their authentic self. Life is too short to not go where your heart leads and I pray that everyone finds what makes them happy and pursues that. I know that I am always home. I love when Rumi said, "I have been a seeker and I still am, but I stopped asking the books and the stars. I started listening to the teaching of my Soul." He went within. Intuition is our superpower. When we stay true to our strengths and calling, we win. Every. Single. Mothereff'n. Time.

Many are stuck doing the same job every day and they hate it. Their intuition may be screaming to make a shift. Physical symptoms may appear, including but not limited to: panic attacks, shortness of breath, lightheadedness, a feeling of uneasiness that follows you everywhere, insomnia, and weight gain, just to name a few. Why do they stay in this state? Because they don't really know themselves. How can someone make a major change if they don't feel confident in who they really are? They don't know which direction to change to. Even worse, they wouldn't know how to champion themselves.

I want you to ask yourself how you show up for *yourself*. Is it a half-ass, slow clap? Or are you mic-droppin' whole-ass'n it? It would be terrifying to think you would have a dream and not double down on yourself. Often people can only tell you what they perceive as their weaknesses and spend their time worrying about them. If you really want to go far, know your strengths and focus on those. If you know yourself and back up your strengths then you can discover your role. Find your way through on your terms from an empowered position. See Sis, I'm here to create my best life and not compete or compare. I believe that's what you're up to as well. If we are at peace, in the mindset of abundance and being inclusive with collaboration and support, we ALL win.

Go get YOUR win.

By staying in YOUR lane.

Go find YOUR peace.

YOUR flow.

And know this:

The blessed don't beef with the miserable.

There are key moments in life that can help you

clarify your divine role. I'll never forget the moment when my stepdad, Larry, told me about my "gift" or what contribution he felt I brought to the world. I was a gallery director for Lightpost Publishing. We sold the works of Thomas Kinkade while in college. It was my mom and step dad's new venture and I begged for the job. They were reluctant because working with family can be tumultuous and I was eighteen years old, an art history minor, and I had no clue what to do in a sales position. I actually turned out to be the top-selling employee. I made over 60K a year by the age of twenty. This was in 1999, nonetheless. I went from sales to management, and as Gallery Director was in charge of selling, hiring, firing, and training new staff. By this time, I had dropped out of college (forfeiting scholarships and grant money) to do this full time. It was also my third season as a teacher and director of my dance studio.

While in a bi-monthly meeting with my stepdad over gallery business, he started to veer off on a tangent about how to start a fire. He should have just laid out crystals, burned some sage and dropped a crystal ball on his desk because I swear it was fucking magical. Literally, though, it was nothing like that. Just me in his office, smoothie in hand, as we discussed sales projections, whether to hire two more employees and fire another one. But it was a landmark moment to hear the words, "Lins, you are an ember carrier."

Say what? I immediately put down my smoothie and leaned in to understand what that meant. Larry proceeded to break down how to start a campfire. He explained that you have to gather the wood and stack it well because its that same wood that keeps the fire going. That you need oxygen to fuel the flame and that you can't forget to keep adding wood to keep the burn hot. Then, to get the fire started, you would need lighter fluid. This will help the wood ignite but what you MUST have to start this whole thing is the spark!

"You are the spark, Lins," he said, "the Ember Carrier!" I was bright-eyed, and overwhelmed, yet enamored as he poured into me a snapshot that fore-shadowed my success many years later. That was recalled with nostalgia. In reality, I just sat there nodding and sipping my smoothie while picturing a campfire with marshmallows roasting. That was defi-nitely a delayed shift making, definitive moment. The spark metaphor deeply resonated with me. I felt like a map was laid out for me. Now, to be fully transparent, I didn't quite shift into this mindset until my late thir-ties. But, on that day, Larry helped embed the concept of who I was so that I would know my strength and understand how to use it. What a million dollar moment!

Once I learned to double down on that strength and shift focus away from my self-perceived weak-nesses, I took off like a rocket. The really beautiful part of it is I get to spark a lot of rockets because I strictly focus on this strength of mine. You will know the moment when you figure out who you really are. I was enlightened back in '99 but I didn't "go within" until later. I chalk it up to my age, ignorance, and lack of experience to really see the depth of that conversation. You may be reading this now wondering if you, too, are an ember carrier. You will immediately think you are, but then find some memory to exemplify how you are not. You see how your mind tricks you? It wants to keep you safe and small. You know your strengths. You know your weaknesses. So focus on what you do best and hire, trade, or delegate the rest so you can step into the ember carrier (or another role) that you truly are.

For those of you who get sweaty when I discuss your "role," please do not get caught up in the terminology. See it as an umbrella instead. I am a mother of five and can't remember the last time I did laundry so I will be the last person on earth to ever assign what your "role" should be. Hindsight definitely creates 20/20 vision. Now that I know what my strengths are, I should have never assumed the "role" of Gallery Director. My strengths were sales, not profit and loss reports. Now here's my nudge: what role are you assuming that really is better left for someone else? What can you hand off today that will allow you to embody your true strength? I'd like to share with you my campfire concept in its entirety and see if anything resonates for you.

To break it down, here's how I compartmentalize your possible role in life (there are many—pick one) based on the campfire analogy:

The ember carrier: the spark—the catalyst that creates the fire. This person sees the bigger picture and knows what needs to happen to set it in motion.

The gatherer: the person who gathers the wood to feed the flames. The Coordinator. Without this step, the fire from one log would eventually die out. This person gathers and connects the right people and/or things together to make shit happen.

The wood: the kindling. the person with structure, a system and always a master plan. The one who is the foundation to the entire fire.

The wind: the person there to fan the flames. The Encourager. The one that champions the growth of the flame in everyone around them.

All of these elements work cohesively to create the success of the fire. When you know who you are, it makes your mission more efficient by collaborating with others who embody strengths opposite of yours. This combination creates cohesiveness in your mastermind gathering. Having one without the other will affect your outcome. To go fast, you can go alone. To go far, you need to go together. Collaboration trumps solo endeavors so find those who skillsets differ from you. The only way to know what you need is by knowing who you are.

How are you showing up in life? How do you need others to show up for you? Just knowing what you need will help you to find it later on when it comes across your path. It takes courage to show up for yourself. An inspiring act of bravery is being bold enough to know your worth and stand in unwavering belief that you deserve a life full of abundance, love, happiness, and authentic relationships. It starts with your thoughts, and no, you are not selfish for wanting this. Yes, it is possible for you. Anything is possible when you have a belief and a standard and follow it with action.

We cannot be inspired into action if our emotions are all over the place. There is a lot of misinformation in this age of fake news and unsolicited advice. I believe this is a time of spiritual awakening for many. Yet we are subjected to labeling more than ever. I see more people labeling their shitty behavior and moods in alignment with their zodiac sign rather than just admitting they have no control over their emotions. Heck, I'm a Leo and married to a Leo. GASP! According to our signs, we would never make a good match. After twenty-six years, we have yet to smother one another in our sleep. We are polar opposite on so many Leo traits which tells me that labeling my husband a Leo when he's not as Leo-y as I, is wildly inaccurate.

When I was a tween, I would find my way to the magazine aisle every time I was at any grocery store. I would swoop up a *Teen Beat,* or even a *Cosmopolitan,* just for the monthly horoscope. It was like a weather forecast of my emotions and love interests, and I believed every vague-ass word I read. Totally fun if the forecast was sunny and cheery. But, what happened when I would read gloom and doom? For example, I thought to myself, "Do I wait for the 5th of November to let my ambitions soar and have none for the first four days of the month?" There are so many variables that really don't tell you anything. No zodiac sign should be your true compass to life even though I still love me some astrological charts. When we live outside our body instead of going within, we are not embodying who we really are. Just because I know a few crazy Geminis doesn't mean they are all crazy. You have to be confident in who you are to combat the shitstorm of information that is thrown your way every day.

When you know who the fuck you are and what you want, you will figure out the how. Though I believe that retrograde is a real thing—like disease, sadness and anxiety are real- by constantly referring to or acknowledging them you are giving them power over you. What you focus on expands. If you let your parents or others tell you who they think you should be, or you spend your days as a chameleon making decisions based on what will make someone else happy, you will emulate the people around you instead of being yourself. There was a time when I felt I wasn't a strong person because I couldn't tell you what my favorite color was. There's no way a judge could be so wishy-washy, right?

I felt that everyone else could give you ONE color that resonated with them. So why couldn't I choose just one color? I'm like a walking mood ring, changing my favorite color as my mood changes. I love pink but resonate with black. I love orange and red but I rarely wear them. And guess what?! That is okay. I'm not a wishy-washy person, I just like variety. I judged myself on this until I just really honored who I am. I am a full-color spectrum kind of gal. I stay true to my core beliefs and mix and match the rest of the details depending on the day. I own it. I own all of it.

If you haven't figured out by now I'll tell you that I love music. Like, *really love music.* Songs speak for me and can explain exactly how I feel even when I don't have the words myself. You just need the right song to time warp you to an experience. It's like a soundtrack to my life. I nudge you to make your own soundtrack rather than being stuck in someone else's movie. Oh, the memories!

I'm talking poolside tanning with my sister in eighth grade listening to "Spring Love" by Stevie B. I remember summer weekends I spent at Santa Cruz Boardwalk whenever I hear the Red Hot Chilli Peppers. Or Mike picking me up for school the first day of junior year when I listen to "Kashmir" by Led Zeppelin. My mind slipped right into the bedroom rocking my babies to sleep while "You Are My Sunshine" was playing at a funeral for a dear friend's mom. They also played, "I Hope You Dance," by Lee Ann Womack, and the memories just kept flowing in. Music transcends the basic experience and evokes a visceral emotion that fuses with that moment.

I can't remember what I did on most random days but if you put a song on, I can time stamp it and remember the moment like yesterday. Every year, my husband and I go somewhere special on our anniversary. Whether it's a drive to San Francisco or hiking in Tahoe, I create a new playlist for the drive. So, now, when we hear a specific song, it sparks a conversation about our time together. You want intimacy that lasts longer than your anniversary weekend, Sis? Make a playlist! Put a time stamp on your personal transformation as well! Play songs that remind you of who you are, or play new songs while making discoveries about yourself. Love punch: stop listening to sad songs when you want to feel empowered. Alexa, play "Groove Thang" by Zhané.

You just have to be you. It's easier than you think! Practice being you if you have to, and be your own guru. Get better at filling yourself with knowledge and putting in the work of healing and growing. Don't sit back and covet others who seem to have their life together in hopes that, through osmosis, you will embody what they portray.

Truth: everyone struggles.

Those who bounce back better after a fall... WINNING

Those who see lessons instead of failures... WINNING

Those who see internal peace as the ultimate success... WINNING

Sis, finding your authentic self will make you shine brightly. Just remember that as you shine, you will attract more darkness. Darkness is always seeking the light and it's hard to shake this feeling when you have lackluster friends. You know the ones. They are missing the whole point of life but always have advice for you. Our mission should be to always add something good to a relationship. Fan the flames of another and help them win, too. Wisdom is built through awareness, not bestowed. We don't truly do anything alone. We really are all in this together. However, you need to release the fake-ass friends. When you allow them to show up authentically but they won't do the same for you, it's time to bounce. Being your own guru means you trust that inner voice inside of you to guide you to the answers that will serve you at your highest level. Love punch: you already know who needs to get dropped, so follow through this time.

My connection to my intuition is strong and I no longer doubt its power. I find my church in the mountains and at my hair salon. Now, if you haven't had a cry fest or felt that holy spirit in the salon, you need to find a new stylist. I talk to Spirit and Spirit speaks back. Usually through my creativity and with messages on how to help other people understand things that I just intuitively know. I have received initiations in this life that have made me comfortable with one foot in the shadow and one in the light. I have someone else's memories burned into my nervous system about being entombed and killed for what (they) believed in. I've stood over my lifeless body while in a meditative state to heal and release trauma in one of my past lives. I can see my guides, one of which is my grandma, Ester, who passed many years ago. She tells me to stop holding my phone so often and I usually feel her presence while in my bathroom. I know that I was my mother's mother before she was ever born to Ester and have spent years releasing and healing trapped emotions, soul contracts and other's energy that I've acquired throughout my life.

I am thankful that we are getting more open and aligned to speak and practice whatever our particular energy work is without harm or judgment. I would love for us to get rid of the word "woo-woo," which means a person readily accepting supernatural, paranormal, pseudoscientific phenomena, or emotion-based beliefs and explanations. Nothing I care about or believe is weird, dark or even cute. It's natural medicine. It's healing the body and trauma that keeps showing up. It's the senses. It's the earth and the elements. It's the moon and the sun and I pray and ask for grace from God and my guides daily. I am a light seeker, I am a healer, I love me some Jesus, and I wear crystals in my bra. Really knowing myself has allowed me to expand in ways I only dreamed of. The world needs the real me and the real you so let it out, and fuck what people think.

Imma good girl with a hood playlist.

A little love and light and a little "go sit and spin."

I'm extremely deep in thought,

yet can be petty when pushed.

I'm both the alpha and the omega.

Both yin and yang.

Pink like Barbie today and emo-ish black errrrthang tomorrow.

The best part of my eternal, oxymoronic energy is that I'm ever evolving, healing, and regenerating so don't paint me inside your little box. I like to color outside the lines whenever possible.

Time to get real!

- How do you show up for yourself?

....

....

....

- How are you showing up in life?

....

....

....

- How do you need others to show up for you?

- Are you the ember carrier, the gatherer, the wood, the kindling or the wind?

Be *willing* to drop old concepts when they no longer *work for you.*

-Lindsey

4
_____

THE HOLY SHIFT

The Holy Shift is essentially becoming more of who you already are. It's not learning another language; it's self-discovery. It's not easy but it's essential for change. Shifting comes in many forms, even in algebra. But, I'm not speaking of transforming parabolas and shifting vertexes.

I'm talking shifting...

- shame to grace
- fear to love
- hustle to flow
- small to unstoppable
- external priority to internal badassery
- problem to solution
- voiceless to messenger
- expectations to personal desires
- restrictive dieting to intuitive eating

- recipe life to master baker

I'm a self-proclaimed professional baker. I've been told that I make the best chocolate chip cookies. I've been wooing my family and friends for years with a recipe from my dear friend, Kerry, who bakes me cookies each year during recital rehearsals. I got her recipe and have been using it ever since. My friends always ask if I'll share my recipe. People assume it's a sacred one, and hope I'd be willing to break the family trust and divulge the deets. I just wish I was next to them to see their faces when I text them a picture of the backside of a Toll House™ chocolate chip bag. Here's the secret: there is no secret. No unique ingredients, no special recipe. Just the one on the back of the morsel bag. I bake these so often that I know the recipe by heart. So much so that I don't even think about a recipe, and I can whip up a batch in 15 minutes! This is from repetition and habit. And guess what? There was a recipe laid out for you as a child, one that you follow today and believe is the best way to lead your best life.

It wasn't a tasty Toll House™ recipe, though. It was a recipe for achieving the American Dream. It was likely made by your parents or grandparents who had the best of intentions to see that you prosper and have more "options" than they ever did. This recipe of what your life was supposed to consist of can also be described as a script. This script was adopted early on and was created to help people arrive safely to retirement. Who actually created this recipe for life-long bliss? Did you know it was indoctrinated into your brain since you were a child by your parents who really didn't have a plan themselves? They just knew they were miserable working their 9-5 jobs so they felt this recipe would give you a bigger, better cookie with more "dough" and choco chips to boot. Now that we are forty plus years in action, we are noticing the need for a massive shift and improvisation to the recipe created by the Baby Boomers.

The shifting has created a divide between the proverbial lifers and the savage rebels. Many have thrived and love this standard recipe for life, while many others approached retirement, feeling they wasted forty years at big corporations that would replace them within three days if they died unexpectedly. I didn't need to research examples to make my point. I know them.

My dad, Robert, in his mid-sixties and four years into retirement, told me that he stayed in his job too long. He is the most loving and devoted father and papa. He took my sister and me to dance class every week, attended or coached every sport we played and made THE BEST Saturday morning breakfasts. He has the most incredible artistic and wood craftsmanship skills. He's built and created all of my sets props for my dance recitals and makes life-size Barbie display boxes for my daughter's 4th birthday party. But, let this be clear, he's a lifer! He worked the same job hauling eggs for an egg plant for over forty years.

The only change was the company's name from small business to big corp. Some of my best memories were riding along with him during summer break. I would bring my skates and roll through the plant and their huge refrigeration storage areas. It had a small family, totally tight nit feel. Company picnics where everyone knew your name. When my dad retired a few years back, he never got a work luncheon celebration, flowers, or a watch. He got a lunch date with a new manager he'd barely known. Now if that isn't the biggest "fuck you" to the loyalty of a lifer, what else is?!

This will not be me, and it doesn't have to be you, either. We've been spoon fed a recipe for a prosperous life, a one size fits all punch list of ingredients, sugar-coated with the best of intentions. In 2019, it's looking more like a busted can of biscuits. Or how my belly looks when my Spanx(TM) don't fit correctly. This universal recipe no longer leaves a yummy taste in my mouth. This recipe is also known as a script. My friend and mentor, Blake Mallen created "Shift the Script" where he has listed all of the "supposed to's" in life that we all just followed and/or deemed as the perfect recipe to the American Dream. Blake's script points out the order in which you are SUPPOSED to:

- Go to school.
- Get good grades.
- Get into college.
- Get a good job.

- Make good money.
- Get married.
- Start a family.
- Save your money.
- Eventually, retire and live a good life.

Blake's TED Talk called, *Shift The Script,* was my validation that I wasn't being rebellious. I was being true to myself because this script no longer works for me. Blake talks about this traditional script and how it's inherently flawed. The most obvious reason is that no two of us are the same, so a "one size fits all" life plan doesn't work. The concept is noble but it's one of those things that has gone unquestioned for so long that it just keeps happening. Meanwhile, college graduates enter their career path drowning in debt. Many end up changing careers because they realized it's not what they really want to do. Others stay because they've already invested the time and money in their choice.

Trying to apply the list on principle skill sets learned via a textbook to real life, when the professor who taught said theories, probably hasn't applied them in twenty years ... issa problem for me. He only teaches it. Like what the actual hell have we been spoon fed to believe is right all these years? For those who went to college and got the credential, certifications, diplomas, masters, and doctorate to thrive in an area of your skillset, I am in AWE of you! We need you! We need teachers, doctors, nurses, lawyers, social workers, therapists, criminologists, etc... who need the fundamental teaching and training to serve those in need.

My stance is not to condemn those who put in the time, took the financial hit and are degreed-up like a badass. My beef is over those who did it with no clue or actual desire to be in their current profession. They did it because they were expected to. They did it because they didn't have any other ideas on what they wanted out of life. They wanted to make their parents proud. Sorry love, but you've been sold a recipe that's not in your highest good. No wonder you're successful yet miserable. May I offer you a shift for your life via a new recipe? It's never too late to add a new flavor to your current one. Just look five to ten years down the road and ask yourself if you'll still want to be in the same profession, and think about what that life would look like. If you're cringing at the thought of it, then it's time to shift your direction. Expose yourself to new experiences or start doing again what you always knew you liked to do but didn't have the courage to move forward with. Take some classes, a night course, take up a hobby and begin planning your next steps in the right direction for YOU.

Now, let's ponder the flip side of this. Some of you just read the last paragraph with a smirk because you, rebel savage, refused to be in this matrix game. You weren't eating those script cookies and you sure as shit weren't going to be in a career that didn't blow your skirt up. Yet, at times, you have questioned your decision. You've chalked it up to being stubborn. You've probably questioned your value because you did a few years at the local jr. college and realized that script just wasn't for you. You know you are better off. Yet that darn script keeps you questioning your choices.

The self-doubt and regrets are not serving you. Take the time to write down your fears as they come up to the surface, and then write a rebuttal for each one to change the vibe to positive. For example, if you're kicking yourself about quitting college because you started a family and needed a break, then make a plan to go back with the end result in focus. Write down all the positive things you've accomplished lately and pat yourself on the back, Sis. You deserve some high fives for taking a few detours. Yet still have a goal that you will now actively pursue.

I'll tell you how I maneuvered my recipe expectations in the hope that this will help put things into perspective for you. I was never pushed to go to college or get good grades. Having friends ready to degree-up just lead me right along with em. Affirmation is a love language of mine, so receiving praise for my determination literally kept me people pleasing for years. I am an achiever, and I wanted to be successful somehow someway, so this script seemed to be the yellow brick road to my future. I really wanted to go to a university. I set my sights on a private college in Orange County, California. I thought it would be perfect to major in Communications, minor in Art History, and audition for dance jobs in LA. My ideal plan was to dance at Disney or in music videos. I'm not gonna lie, getting an acceptance letter from them was a big deal to me.

But, then, HOLY SHIFT, my parents separated unexpectedly. I went from California University dream'n to varsity blues with overwhelm and depression of circumstance and felt it best to just stay home. I was a lost pup my senior year. I now look at my pictures and just see overwhelm on my face. What I needed was a mentor, a counselor, a strong leader. I needed a mother figure to encourage me. My dad really tried but he was hurting and in survival. That fall, I went to a small University close to home. Looking back, I'm glad I did. Had I left for college, I doubt I would have my dance studio, have taught thousands of dancers and created a dance force in my small hometown. I never danced in a music video but I got to choreograph for one. I never auditioned for Disney but now my dancers dance in the parades there. Holy Shift! I am grateful for this perspective.

My next major shift came during my junior year in college when I was assisting a professor with his project. We were discussing my GPA, how my lack of focus in a class and the resulting failing grade. It was the first time not on the Dean's List and I would have to retake the course. Working one job to pay my bills, teaching dance at night to feed my passion, and having a full course load was taking its toll. My professor's words were a sincere shifting quip that I'll never forget.

He said, "Well, if you want to be a professor, making $70k a year like me, you need to focus on school." Now, I'm not a skilled mathematician but I quickly realized that I was making close to his salary per year selling artwork & teaching at my studio. That was the moment I realized I was wasting my time stressing over Dean's Lists when I was selling artwork, dancing my dreams, and now living with Mike in our first home. My dreams of being a college professor or news anchor shifted to buying and selling artwork, opening smaller galleries with new and original works of art, teaching dance, and recital production.

So I quit college. I just stopped going. Just like that. Lost my communication department scholarship for the following semester and my grants (thanks to my parents' divorce and financial ruin, I qualified for school for free) and said deuces to education. Can you say, "SHIFTED AF?!"

Self-evolution requires a shift in mindset. You have to be willing to learn new things because you do not and cannot know it all. You have to be willing to drop the old concepts when they no longer work for you. You have to be willing to see your current situations for what they are and say, "I do not want to do that anymore," and get over worrying what other people will think of your decisions.

Damn, I wish I believed this to be true when I dropped out of college. I was ashamed of it for years. All my close friends were attending a college, so even though I was making significant income, not having a degree was messing with my inner value system. I was so miserable, but I had to drop that plate. Mind you, I was nineteen years old with zero mentorship. Do you know how hard it was to find a mentor in 1998? I was barely 20 and it was the era of dial-up internet. Utilizing the internet like we do today wasn't even a dream yet.

I used to dial into my AOL site, then get in the shower while the page loaded. Today, my kids (and myself included) lose our shit when the streamed movie pauses for 2.5 seconds. There was no Google or Facebook, not even MySpace! Limewire was about to launch and give all our computers an STD in exchange for free music. Online retail shopping was only a dream. Alexa, play "Juicy" by The Notorious B.I.G. And no YouTube! Gasp! No free access to YouTube or podcast training from mentors and thought leaders like Gary Vee, Tony Robbins, Mel Robbins, Gabby Bernstein or John C. Maxwell. I went to bookstores to buy Napoleon Hill and Wayne Dyer and weight loss books by Susan Powter. Remember her? She had a shaved head and wanted you to "stop the insanity!" Me too, Sis... Me too!

I became a keen observer and networked with successful entrepreneurs who were buying artwork from me at the gallery. Through sales and interactions, I realized very quickly that being successful on paper doesn't equal happiness. Customers came in to buy five paintings and requested that I set them up in their mansion. Then, a year later, they requested to get them appraised because they were divorcing. By the age of twenty, I was traveling to Monterey to train on sales as one of the top-selling consultants in the national chain of signature galleries. I was flying by the seat of my pants. I was just an excited kid who loved art and sharing it with people. I really found myself mesmerized by the pomp and circumstance, the howty-towty and glam that came with art showing, and galas and parties with Silver Oak wine and Cuban cigars to celebrate massive sales.

I also learned that even though I admired some people in the gallery world, idolizing them for the money they made, the talent they possessed, and the knowledge they had was a sure fire way to disappointment. Wealthy and famous people are humans with human experiences. We are the same. One pant leg at a time, people! Pedestal admiration, or seeing another person as superhuman, isn't fair to them or to you. See them for how they overcome obstacles rather than for the car they drive. See them for mastering a skill set rather than their villa in Capri, Italy. Revere them for their integrity and family values rather than their private jet.

Before I was twenty years old, I quickly learned that I hold the pen to my future. No one will have my back like I have my own. Not even family. I was running with the big dogs though, learning some significant life and business lessons while all my friends were still living at home and going to the local junior college or off to University. I was most definitely attending the school of hard knocks but I will tell you now that the juice was worth the squeeze. I'm stronger for it because the shifts I made were in my divine favor and significance in my evolution. I could have never learned all that from a textbook.

If you are pondering a shift in career, I want you to be courageous in starting anew. It's your time. You know it! I'm just that little nudge you think you need. But, honestly, you've been ready. For those pondering adding a side gig, just do it!

That blog? *Go write it.*

That podcast? *Go start it.*

That YouTube channel? *Go film your first video.*

That Etsy Store? *Go fill it.*

Every next level of your life will demand a different version of you. We often forget that because we are in a constant state of survival mode, remaining true to ourselves is a process of daily awareness. It's one thing to admit you want to make a change. It's another to acknowledge that you NEED a change. Life happens though, and we are constantly being torn away from our thought process by the daily needs of our household. Kids have homework, soccer, volleyball, cheer, and you need to get groceries for dinner with a toddler in tow. Once your kids are home from practice, homework done, fed, bathed and in bed; you sit down with your spouse and think "WTF, it's only Tuesday!" You're tired, Sis! So it's easy to forget that you planned to brainstorm ideas tonight for your next blog post. It's no surprise you give zero fucks about completing your application to your next certification training.

My tip for you is to time block. Just as you block out timeframes for work, your hair appt, your children's activities, you must time block your reading, writing, journaling, podcasting listening, and business plan creating...things. Schedule it in when you have breaks at work, or get up an hour early before it's time to get the kids up for school. I will never nudge or suggest that you to wake up at 5:30 AM to be more productive. My bestie, Jen does this because it works for her. I do my best work at night. Let's all agree to disagree, be big girls and just find blocks of time where we can get productive shit done.

Can we also bow our heads and take a knee for all the time wasted on the scroll-hole of social media, watching T.V., and texting hilarious gifs to our squad? Be proactive and creative about finding times that work for YOU to time block and follow through. Stay committed even when you don't feel like it. You are developing a new habit and by staying flexible about *the when,* you'll always find *the how.* Your biggest hurdle will be to stay positive while changing up the schedule when the tide comes in and something doesn't go as planned. Build your mental momentum and before you know it, you won't be derailed by distractions. I'm obsessed with my vision and goals. So when I encounter setbacks, I seek the solution, not the nearest exit sign. Alexa, play "Obsessed" by Mariah Carey.

Before you get too far in your shift, though, be

careful not to confuse being authentic with being intractable. Sometimes, we avoid certain activities or thoughts because we think, "Nah, this is not me." Be quick to check in because what wasn't you last year may be you right now.

The current version of us – in this time, place, and circumstance – is constantly downloading and in return, desiring more upgrades. Judging your own evolution parallels shaming yourself for breathing. You were made for more, so questioning your worthiness to have it is, once again, a massive block to your blessings. The world is ever changing and we have yet to reach the full potential of our authentic self. In that sense, if we never experiment and work towards our next level, then are we truly ourselves? Or just a fragment of what we could be?

It's time we raise our standards. No more settling and using all of our energy to stay stuck. Once you see what's possible, you can't unsee it. When you start living life the way you want, you can't ever go back. We are not the survival of the fittest. We are a survival of the nurtured. It's not about conquering anymore. It's about connecting, collaborating and encouraging everyone to rise up together.

Either way, we never have to lose. I never lose. It's either a blessing or a lesson! The following quote by Rick Warren has always resonated with me, as it describes a major shift I made: "At some point in your life you must, decide whether you want to impress people or influence people."

There are seven aspects of my life that I shifted in order to move from "impressing" to "impacting." I want to share them with you now so you can also make the shift.

***

GRATITUDE

Being grateful for what I have rather than focusing on what I don't have keeps me in a state of abundance. When you can grasp the true meaning of RICH (Realizing I Create Happiness), you will have a shift! You have to keep training and retraining your brain to focus on gratitude. This will help you focus 90% of your time on solutions and only 10% on the problems. A grateful heart is a magnet for miracles.

Gratitude:

- Makes you happier by triggering positive memories
- Makes you more optimistic, which in turn improves your health
- Increases physical and mental well being, which boosts energy
- Boosts your business by helping you network more, be more productive
- Motivates you to delegate more so you can be a mom-boss!

The only difference between the "haves" and the "have-nots" is their ability to quiet their mind monkeys and take action to be a little more than they were yesterday. Gratitude is an intentional practice that can shift your energy to work for you instead of against you. You get so much more accomplished that way.

Go out of your way to notice things you are grateful for, even if it seems silly at first. If you've never done this and you want to start small, make a goal to notice five things you are grateful for each day. Write them down in a gratitude journal if you like to write. Or record your voice on your phone if you're more of an auditory person. They can be anything as basic as the color of your sheets, the smell of your coffee, or the beautiful sunset you were able to view for a few minutes that day. Use your five senses to come up with five things you are grateful for, and make it a routine every morning or evening. Hey Sis, I promise you'll be delighted when you realize what amazing things you can come up with each day! Be creative. Be you. Notice what stands out to YOU and you'll see that there are plenty of things to be grateful for.

Faith

Faith is making the decision to believe that life is

happening for you. Not to you. It's trusting that the right people come and go at the right time for your greatest good. It's seeking that inner voice that lets you know you are loved and supported.

Do you feel fated? Destined to struggle? Fatal? Does hopelessness creep in your head and leave you utterly exhausted and weak in the knees?

Or …

Do you feel faithful? Do you rise above the noise? Do you know you are designed perfectly and made for more than what you've settled for?

It's your choice. Make a conscious decision to believe in something good for your life. You may have to dig deep. Or you may already know this. Think back to a time when someone believed in you, and remind yourself of the message and their good intentions. If you don't remember a time when someone believed in you, ask yourself what you would say to a child about the age you were when you were let down in some way. Tell that child now what she needs to hear, and believe your own advice! After all, you'd want your daughter, your niece or the neighbor girl to do the same. Believe in yourself to find the answers you've been looking for. Believe in your ability to dream, create, and build something greater than yourself. Have faith that if you don't have all the answers, they'll come to you. You've got this, Sis!

Focus

Your attention is a powerful investment. Whatever keeps your focus is taking your time.

Your time is valuable. It's also your most precious commodity because it's nonrenewable.

Spend your time wisely. Time is never given freely. It is always an exchange with your energy. Use it to make a positive difference for someone else or for feeding your soul. Your focus also amplifies whatever you can't take your mind off of. Basically whatever you are staring at or feeling relentlessly is growing stronger. Ideally, it's something you want to grow.

Channel your attention to the things that matter most to you, and don't let anything else—the noise—get in. Use whatever tools work best for you. If music helps you get into the zone, crank it up! If you're a more visual person, make a flowchart or to do list or even a vision board. Find a way that speaks to you and channel your focus to the things that matter most. Those things are what will help build your dream.

Get rid of any clutter around you that doesn't serve your purpose, literally and figuratively. Do you have things in your house that no longer serve you? Get rid of them! They're sucking your energy away from what matters most. Do you have people in your life that always bring you down? Maybe it's time to re-evaluate your friendships and say goodbye to the ones that are doing more harm than good. Communicate with the ones you want to keep around that just need a little refocusing adjustment. You might need to confront someone who is just not getting it and clutters your space with their unhelpful expectations. Get used to saying things like, "That doesn't work for me." Or "I'm good, thanks." You don't owe any explanations to anyone, and these quick responses do the job of politely declining and moving on. Decluttering your life so you can focus on your intention will propel you forward in ways you never thought possible.

BODY LOVE

Your value is not measured in pounds. If you base your worth on how you look or what you weigh, it's time to shift your inner critic. Maybe your mother didn't love herself. Maybe your father didn't respect women. Maybe someone said or did something that left you feeling negatively about your body. Whatever blueprint you have been using can be shifted! Here's another love punch: it is not your fault if you were abused or have childhood trauma but it is most definitely your responsibility to heal from it. As you begin to explore healing your negative self-talk and not only accepting but loving your physical body, you just might see entire limiting, negative walls disappear around you. Self-acceptance carries a powerful confidence that sets people at ease with themselves. Loving your body is a fundamental part of this new shift. If you want to impress, look great for a day. If you want to impact, be great and leave a legacy.

When you love your body, everybody will notice! They'll want to get to know you and find out what your secret sauce is. They'll want to be around you because you have something they know they don't have, but they can't put a finger on exactly what it is. Or they may just want to be around you because your love for yourself is creating a beautiful glow that surrounds you, and they love to bask in the warmth of it.

GET SPI-RICH-UAL

This is the richest rich for me. To feel connected to Source is one of the wealthiest experiences we can have.

Wealthy in love.

Wealthy in friendship.

Wealthy in health.

Wealthy in experience.

Wealthy in parenthood.

Wealthy in time freedom.

Wealthy in how you pay it forward

Ain't no poverty in spirituality, baby.

Your vibe can take you from zero to hero over time. Now add in some posture, alignment, finding your niche, solving for X, and massive action ... and it can take you to the Promised Land.

You can get your spi-RICH-ual on whether you are religious or not. Go to your favorite praying spot, your bedroom, in your shower, favorite beach, or to your favorite hiking spot. Go wherever you feel connected to Source, and pour your heart out. Send out all your intentions and then listen to the sounds in your house or the sounds of nature. Meditate on all the possibilities and don't hold back. Something good is coming your way, and you'll know it when you feel it. Within this tranquil space, you'll find yourself more open to receiving the answers you've been looking for. Let the Universe provide, and don't be afraid of, or worry about how this will happen. You are connected with the Divine and what needs to happen will happen.

PRESENCE

Living in the now is a mindful practice. Since most of us are obsessed with our phones, being present in the moment is hard AF. The year my mom was diagnosed with early onset dementia, I was diagnosed with an autoimmune disease. I've spent the last seven years rewiring my internal blueprint of anxiety and restructure my empathic abilities to strengthen instead of paralyze and hinder my own healing. I didn't know how I was making the goiter in my throat disappear, but the desire and belief I could heal was there. They say when the student is ready, the teacher will appear.

My mother's diagnosis was how I learned about the power of living in the present moment. She no longer cared about her future and rarely mentioned her past. She was completely in the moment, no recollection or care of time. Watching my mom mentally and physically deteriorate kept me in a state of panic for the 1st year she was placed in full-time care. I learned that by focusing on my breath I could stop panicking over the future or feeling depressed about the past. I brought myself back into my actual body and in the present moment. Being in awareness, calling yourself out on your own bullshit of things that keep your focus, and creating time to just breathe allows the shifts to take place.

FORGIVENESS

I cannot heal my mother, and I'll never get closure now with the state of mind she's in. She can't write out her own name, cannot call me every day like she once did, recall what day it is or that she always wanted to travel the world. I can, however, heal myself. I heal through forgiveness from unspoken hurt and anger when she divorced my dad and left me to establish her new life. I will never get closure with her on so many things. Yet now I feel it, I heal it, and I release it. And that's all I can do.

The art of healing is not linear. It is filled with ups and downs, twists and turns, two steps forward, three steps back kind of cha-cha-cha movement. My mother loves me and is so proud of me, yet she wasn't the mother I needed emotionally. Though these two truths coexisting may seem unfathomable, they are my truth. You not speaking your truth (however fucked up or sad it may be) is the very same reason you have loops. I am not dishonoring my mother. I am honoring my truth. But instead of continuing to blame or resent her, I shifted to have the most gratitude for her. Because if she was everything I ever needed, I wouldn't have half the drive I have today. I would be half the mother I am right now.

I forgive her for leaving me but I'm grateful for her coming back once she found her joy again. I knew I truly forgave her when I put myself into her shoes and felt her loneliness and desire for more. How can I begrudge someone trying to navigate their life through uncharted waters? I was angry about not having a choice and not being a priority at that time. But holding on to anger wasn't serving me. I let it go. You must let go or be dragged down with the resentments and expectations you place on others. Your true sense of self-worth and joy will come from unexpected places if you allow it. If I allowed myself to wade in my emotional cesspool of should-haves, could-haves, and what-ifs, along with the daily rants of "why me?!", I would surely have drowned by now. I have made the decision to choose joy over sadness. Flow over hustle. Gratitude over guilt. Faith over fear. And simply to forgive. Forgiveness allowed me to love my mother unconditionally and heal the little fifteen-year-old girl who felt lost and hurt so long ago.

Your child's success and failures are not your responsibility. But your unconditional love for them is.

-Lindsey

5

PARENT ON PURPOSE

Mom'n ain't easy, yo! Being a parent is the biggest mind screw of my life. Mike and I planned to create a large family and we are pretty proud of how we've handled the pressure of 5 children thus far. It hasn't been without trial and error and some tears along the way. We find ourselves giddy to go on dates alone. Then spend the majority of our time talking about the kids. We get annoyed with all their toys and hobbies cluttering our counters, dirty clothes left on the floor and dishes left in the sink but when one child is gone overnight, the entire house feels empty.

Parenting can be the most rewarding and satisfying role of your life if you learn to make some shifts in how you perceive this responsibility. Making a shift in my parenting from "expecting perfection with all eyes on me" to "let's love them unconditionally and example kindness while they navigate their own way" helped me release a desire for an unattainable standard I set long before I had kids. Shifting my need of perception of perfection to just being a better person and really embodying unconditional love really just allowed my kids to be kids.

I chose the verb "practice" because unless you are Mother Teresa, you can flip from unconditional to conditional love real quick while parenting. Mama, this isn't a judgment call. It's a reality for many. Now, if you are a new mommy, you have yet to feel the frustration when nail polish gets spilled on the carpet. When your child lies right to your face. Or you worked hard to buy them a pair of Nikes and they lose them within a week. Be prepared. It will happen. Being angry or disappointed with your child is inevitable. It's how to approach and handle the anger when it happens that matters. I call this parenting on purpose because it's just that. It's being conscious of your role as the caretaker and provider rather than a dictator instilling fear. Or manipulator for their love and constant adoration. I want to share how I shifted and eased into parenting with intention and how this has made a positive impact on my children and our flow at home.

Take what you can from where you are right now knowing my story is just that. Mine. At the very least, know that your growth will soar if you take what you've learned and teach someone else. Listen to your intuition and lean in on what helps you and move along from what you don't agree with. That's all I can ask from you. Parenting is merely offering unconditional love to a miniature version of yourself that has its own soul and emotions. You'll spend the rest of your days encouraging them to do their best while loving themselves and to follow their dreams. Gawd, I sound like a Hallmark™ branded punch list, but am I right? Why does this have to be so difficult? Two words: expectations and baggage.

Once we release and heal old wounds stemming from our own childhood, it's easier to hold space for growth rather than holding onto anger because your marriage leaves you feeling lonely/ your mother may have been neglectful/ your dad always working and favored your sibling more (type of) wounds. Whatever internal trauma loop you are refusing to heal, is the very reason we, as parents, have a tendency to put ourselves on autopilot.

Purpose-driven parenting takes us out of autopilot and restores our ability to create a new path. This new way is how we nurture and also react to the curveballs that life throws our way. There are so many more aspects to it, by that, I mean parenting on purpose is a never-ending responsibility. Just as I won't stop worrying or being a support system to my children when they are adults and raising their own family. I will forever strive to be a good listener, allow my kids to be who they are, and not nitpick every little thing they do because it could've been done better (aka, my way.) Not having a hovering mother of my own, I found I became one myself. If I had to swallow my own words of micromanagement, I'd have gagged out long ago.

Holding space for the youth we are raising to safely expand and grow gets much easier when we learn to do the same for ourselves. It starts with us. Your elders will tell you what to do from their own projections, traumas and limiting beliefs. The moment you realize that most adults are usually full of shit and have no clue how to effectively communicate in their own lives, you'll be in the utmost peace of mind to lean into your own intuition. The unfortunate truth is that most of us have no idea what we're doing. We are just winging this parenting gig.

But, what does that mean for the younger generations who are being led by us "wingers?" We are supposed to prepare them for a world we aren't even prepared for. Most navigate through life as if on a hamster wheel, rarely looking up to see where they are or how they got there. I struggled with this until I finally stopped, woke up and took a look around. I took a hard look at my tactics and strategies and looked at how my kids were doing with what I was giving them. Turns out having five kids who are completely different in how they give and receive love, and who need and handle discipline differently can be overwhelming when you choose to stay in autopilot.

Parenting from wherever we are personally in life makes sense when we feel really great about how things are going. But if this isn't the case then why on earth would we not try to learn a new way for ourselves so that we have something that actually works to teach our kids? I mean, we all know an unhappy, stressed out parent who resents the place they are in and refuses to learn anything new about themselves or parenting. They believe their child can model the good and expand from the bad. It's the "do as I say not as I do" mindset. Parents, it's time to SHIFT and learn what makes our child "tick" rather than reacting to when they tick you off. Learn their love language and what motivates them. Understand that their success and failures are not your responsibility. But your unconditional love for them is.

Be a leader for your children. Leaders do not command. Commanding is reactionary and, frankly, lazy. Parenting has never been about how to control tiny humans. It's about being their mentor. Their example. Sharing and communicating along the way. Growing yourself to be a solid foundation for your child is hard. Helping your child do the same is a privilege. As parents, we owe it to our children to continue becoming the best version of ourselves. The trick is to accomplish this while staying present and without shaking their foundation.

Back to the plates metaphor. We have a lot of plates spinning and we don't want to drop the parenting plate in the process. Remember, all the plates we have chosen are equally important if we have chosen them well and taken out the ones we don't need. Divide your time equally between your own personal goals and your parenting responsibilities, and delegate or let your kids discover things on their own when necessary. We can't let our own plates fall. We have to become someone who is not only who we would want to follow but who we'd want our children to learn from and model in their own way. It's a constant checking in of self, auditing, correcting, and juggling process.

We teach our kids what they need to know so that this learned independence gives them a platform to take flight. Like a mama bird, we toss them up into the air and they spread their wings, learn to tie their own shoes and, hopefully, file their own taxes. True leaders make themselves unnecessary. They work themselves out of a job. And while you will never stop having the job of being their parent, there will come a day when you will not be there to catch their fall. Doing everything for our kids won't give them a chance to fully experience life. They need to be able to go out and succeed and fail without us there, waiting in the near distance, holding a first aid kit. Remember, great leaders measure their greatness by their absence. What happens in your absence is your legacy. Sometimes parenting gets confused with wanting to be needed. This type of codependency is emotionally crippling to young adults. Love Punch: your kids don't need to hear about your shitty day, your excuses for being late or even worse, your money and relationship issues.

I recall that my mom always drove me to school late. I would arrive to class, sit at my desk, literally shaking with anxiety. I felt responsible for her happiness and placed the blame for her inability to get ready on time as my fault. Even though I swore to myself that I would not do that to my kids, I found myself ranting in the car when we were running late to school or annoyed when they wanted me to braid their hair before I could get ready myself. I had to self-audit and retrain my reactionary instinct that was modeled throughout my childhood. I had to shift from projecting blame to lesson learned and strive for better time management.

This type of self-check is paramount for your growth as a person and your legacy as a parent. Many of us know that how it's going down at home is usually replicated in our other environments. Our children take it to school and we take it to work. It also shows in our relationships. That's why it's important to show our kids how to act respectfully, be kind and to enforce boundaries when necessary. Model good behavior, be humble and take care of yourself emotionally and physically. Not only will you benefit but so will they because they'll repeat that for themselves later in life. To know better is to do better.

If your idea of a healthy, active lifestyle isn't displayed by your child, all you can do is take comfort knowing that you showed them. I want my kids replicating a life that is filled with joy. So I must show them how to say no when they need to, and yes to what's right for them. Not me, but them. I strive to communicate with them often and let them know they can come to me if they need help in a crisis. If something happened to my children and their first reaction is "My mom is gonna be so mad!" rather than "I'm in trouble, I need to call my mom." I would know I need to do some things differently. If they have a safe place to ask the questions they need to ask and a positive role model to look up to, they will have a much easier time navigating through struggle and relationships.

I believe that success without a successor is failure. Or a hard lesson for a parent. Legacy should be in more than buildings, programs, and projects you do for your career. Your legacy should also be present in people. Especially your kids. When you are imagining your future, think a bit further down the line and explore what will happen after you're gone.

Are you teaching your kids to sustain the same healthy principles you embody today? Do you want them to experience the same marriage or friendship experiences that you currently have? Or are you busting your ass to solely provide a lifestyle where every material need is met rather than emotional needs nurtured? Or will all your hard work and wisdom that you've gained over the years go with you to the grave? Future generations will benefit from the legacy that you build if you include them in it. However, including your children in your poor choices and self-sabotaging ways is a sure fire way to create trauma for them that they later need healing from. What you model becomes their way and what you endure creates their standard.

While I think it's a goal in life to remain close with my daughters, I choose to have best friends that are more my age for now. Now, don't get defensive if you call your daughter your bestie. I love the term of endearment. However, the trend of speaking your personal issues in front of your kids who cannot begin to compartmentalize or fully empathize your struggle exposes them to problems they are not ready to solve. That's why you are the adult. Love punch: dial a friend your age to complain to and stop using your teenager as your sounding board. Welcome to parenting where you must rise up to leadership and literally lead-YOUR-ship.

Let me tell you about how I shifted from squandering my lessons learned to creating exponential blessings in my home. There's an old saying that goes, "A man chasing after two rabbits rarely catches one." Boy, have I chased a few rabbits at once! I was in a constant tailspin, throwing my back out and experiencing stress headaches for weeks at a time. My health had so many personalities that I didn't know who I was going to be each morning. I don't even recognize myself in pics from my twenties. I was stressed out and just pissed off all the time.

It caused inflammation, swelling, and some major brain fog. I didn't know about the value of leveraging my time, asking for help or sharing responsibility. I was at war with myself, feeling my value as a mother required me to be THE DEAL to my babies. If I wasn't satisfying their every need, my perceived worth was negatively affected. I was an absolute martyr. That martyr mindset is so sneaky because, at first glance, it looks like good intention. Your intentions are indeed pure, wanting to be there for everything and everyone, self-sacrificing, overachieving, the Pinterest-perfect mom. I can't blame you. I wanted to be the deal. So much so that Mike and I spent over twenty hours working on Maryn's Under 6 soccer team banner over a period of three days. Like it was our JOB! She could have cared less about the banner and, truthfully, it was uglyAF but I was so determined to be a great soccer mom that I turned into a crazy person. So not worth the sweat, tears, and burns from the glue gun. I never again offered to make a team banner.

What I know now is that it takes a village to raise a well-rounded child. Unless you let go of all the perfectionism and isolating behavior, it's going to be just you in the end. No one has time for your insecurity and overzealous need for accolades. Your kids just want your attention and could give two shits for the 10 layered birthday cake or soccer team banner. Your quest for wooing those around you will burn you out quick and your vibes run far and wide, mama. Your family feels it. Time to check in with what energy you're putting out there and redirect it toward what's important. What's important to me is a peaceful and happy home. My intention of being the overachieving mom for my peers shifted to a mother that provided a home and relationship for my children in hopes they won't need therapy for as adults. (The jury is still out on this one.)

If you have a child, you may relate to how big the gap can be between how you think things will be and how they actually are. It's the "If it's going to be done right, then it's gotta be done by ME" mentality and really thinking *you solo* can do everything. Same as the ideation following conception that you will nurse your baby for the first year minimum, use cloth diapers instead of disposable, not let your kids have an iPad or play with toy guns, or eat anything processed. Oh, and read to them. Every. Single. Night. Yeah, I had these notions too, Sis! I was the perfect mom before I had kids.

I stuck to my core values on most of my parenting standards but I had to give up the "no guns" rule for my third baby, Beau. He would bite down his genetically modified chicken strip into the shape of a gun and pretend it was a weapon at dinner. It was then I realized that by trying to live up to a standard or worry what others may think of my children's behavior was utterly exhausting. Today, I'm all about having an open mindset and a code of ethics for my standards in parenting and business but without the crazy second-guessing of my decisions. Knowing when to bend so you don't break is paramount. Respecting our parenting uniqueness makes all the difference because let's face it, everyone thinks their child is somehow superior, even cuter, than others.

Our boys, Beau and Jett, love guns. They love

things action, blood, destruction, and things that go boom. Alexa, play "Cars That Go Boom" by L'Trimm. This doesn't make them violent. In fact, they are very kind little humans who will appease their little sister and play hide and go seek on her demand. What I've learned from being a mom to boys is that when you give people freedom and let them take some ownership in what they like to do rather than managing their every move, you will find that most thrive. This is how I run my home as well. In my house, everyone has room to grow and learn— including Mike and myself. If you let people *be* who they are then it's much easier to *see* them for who they are rather than who you think they ought to be. Some children need their flames fanned to keep the fire. Some just need more wood or structure to thrive. No one needs a dictator telling them how their flame should burn. Telling them what to like or how to think, what religion is bad and who is worthy of love is exclusive and a lack-mindset. I strive to focus on abundance, inclusivity and a come as you are method.

Mamas, I feel your hearts. You have work you need to finish, things to clean, lunches to pack, maybe a parent or grandparent you help with. Your children have homework deadlines, they need to be driven to boy scouts, dance, karate, and the band's spring show-case. You have one child being bullied, a toddler who won't eat dinner, no one has bathed yet and you are so frustrated and tired that you seek solace by having a good cry in the shower. By Friday, you are emotionally

WIPED out, you haven't gotten any good sleep, the new trainer at the gym is kicking your ass, your side gig is ramping up and you don't have proper time to focus on it.

All you really want is to come home from work, soak in a mineral salt bath, and get your booty slapped more than once a week by your man. But you're too tired and you are starting to question your sanity. (Or is this just me?) Mind you, the weekend is here and, now, it's off to games and birthdays and baby showers... like, it's a perpetual calendar of obligations and celebrations that you love to hate. Truth, I want to change my religion during the holidays just so I can slow down and not even celebrate, kinda shit. I'm not that mom who wants to go to every practice or party. Nothing gets me more excited than canceled plans! If the weather is too cold or too hot, you can expect me to sit in it and complain. This doesn't mean I don't love watching my kids play sports or going to my niece's birthday party. It just means I no longer love forcing my calendar with all the celebratory things or four soccer games on a Saturday in 100-degree heat. I'm not a bad mom. I'm human. And you're human and we are over the overwhelm.

What I'm asking you to do is to stop and be present in the moment to savor the season you are in NOW. No longer speaking of "when the kids get older it will be easier" because love punch: it doesn't get easier. It gets harder! I'll take a tantrum from a two-year-old over letting my sixteen-year-old drive herself around independently any day of the week. I'll take doing 2nd-grade homework, which I utterly hate, versus seeing my adult child go through a divorce. Longing for an ideal situation in your future rather than enjoying what you have now is a sure fire way to regret. Time to shift the nostalgia of the future for the current affairs of the now.

Savoring your season in parenting also bridges the gap to your career season. Sis, I know you can feel the isolation and anxiety that you might be missing out on your big break AKA boss babe moment when you're living that mom life. Know that you can begin at any time on your own to do list when you're ready. Don't rush your body and your precious moments with your baby to prove to someone else that you are a hard worker. On the flip side, your family is not going to fall apart because your career goals make it on the family calendar.

In fact, ultimately, you are teaching everyone something very critical. You are teaching them that they are important by acknowledging you are important, too. We can't tell our kids to go after what they want in life while we sit and chew on sunflower seeds at their baseball tournament twenty weekends of the year. And they also play two other sports. To then tell their adult children they gave up everything for them, it's not empowering, it's devastating and creates guilt for them. So martyr like of you, Sis! All I ever wanted was to be a mom, to be impactful, and have success with significance by doing what I loved. And that's where I'm at today. I've had to fight for it. I've had to put my goals aside while in my newborn season. I've had to revamp and create schedules and delegate to handle the work. I've also had to give up the need to be THE DEAL while doing so. If you have a dream, don't let your children's schedule keep you from reaching it. They should be your motivation. Not your excuse.

What I know from having my children is that my focus and attention will peak and pit based on the season that I am in. There have been many opportunities I've not taken due to my lack of time to really put in the effort needed. I've also missed out on many mom moments while building my empire. I've never regretted either. Here's a secret: YOU AREN'T MISSING SHIT! You aren't missing your epic run or opportunity to SLAY! What you are missing is your current joy. What you are missing is connectedness with your babies and your tribe. Your children are only little once, so it's never the wrong move to be very intentional about the time you spend with them. There will be a day you put your toddler down and never pick them up again.

What I want to shift in you is your focus of perceived perfection and release the FOMO (fear of missing out). Release the anxiety of not getting to do what you want to do *when you want to do it*. Shift to the flow that says you'll do it when you have the opportunity to do so. You are a mom and, therefore, contracted out according to age or special needs of your child. Knowing that everyone is different so comparison is a waste of time. Motherhood is an opportunity, one of the most meaningful opportunities we can have but often leaves us feeling defeated and unfulfilled from constant comparison.

Shift your mindset from "I have to take the kids to dance" to "I get to take my kids to a class they enjoy." The key word is "get to" instead of "have to." Martyrs *have to*, grateful moms *get to*. Shift from "What will the other moms think?" to "This is my reality and opinions hold zero weight." Shift from "My child is so dramatic" to "My child is allowed to have a bad day and it doesn't help by telling them to snap out of it." These are subtle shifts in my behavior that I know will impact my children long term. My kids only get one childhood, I want to give them one with unconditional love, attention, and experiences. I am shifting generational behavior that was not in my highest good to focus on purposeful intentions for my children to adopt and hopefully implement with their future families. Legacy work is powerful and goes beyond the realm of wealth principles when you are parenting on purpose.

6

We create the culture we live in.

-Lindsey

6

_____

BOLD BUSINESS

The most important legacy I will leave is my lasting impression on my children. Our moment to shine as "Mom" and CEO of our household is a top position. Alexa, play "Dear Mama" by Tupac. However, you can be a loving mom and still be bold in your business outside the home. I align with grit and grace as the two staples in my business. The grit is my unwavering determination to hold clear sight of my vision. Grace is my attitude while in pursuit of it. I hope that you'll get out of the trees long enough to see the forest, the vast landscape that it really holds.

Don't let those who are in a different season of life or seem to be moving up fast on the success ladder make you feel insignificant. Your dreams are real and attainable. If you don't believe this, you aren't really committed to the time it will take to achieve them. These are bold words, but Sis, this is bold business we are talking about. No one is coming to save you. This is great news! This means your success is not determined by anyone else. You can go as far and as high as you want to.

You must fight for what's yours and enjoy the journey along the way. When I say fight I don't mean to fight others. I mean to fight that part of you that wants to hold you back, keep you safe from risk-taking and potentially falling flat on your face. The part of you that strives to keep you comfortable means well but it cannot come with you while you are building your dream. It will be too afraid. Enjoying the journey means enjoying the little things. Celebrating the small wins. Finding reasons to laugh or just laughing for no reason at all. This attitude of grace will keep you fluid.

Grit will help you hold fast to your vision to see it through. The clearing of the clouds and the turbulent flight making way to a clear sky and a picturesque sunset. It's a breathtaking ride. Also, a gentle reminder that life is not all clear skies and smooth rides. Having a huge dream requires GRIT and working well with people to see it through. When you're in the thick of it and you're building, there can be a lot of voices inside your head. You have to have the grit to know which voices serve you so you can surrender the ones that don't. Even outsiders will voice their concerns and mean well but not everyone can see what you see. Remember this is your vision, you are the captain of this ship. If things are not looking good and you are receiving a lot of fearful input, you have to be clear-headed enough to make the call to go forward and own it.

Celebrate the small wins but don't take your foot off that gas pedal. Some people tend to stop and graze when they hit a new level or milestone in their business. They may have been laser-focused, working like a champion up until that point, and then they got to the top and became complacent. Complacency is the silent killer of leadership. Leaders actually do the most harm when they think they've arrived. If you want to lead, you need to remain consistent in serving your people. Leadership requires both an aerial view and a front line (hands-on approach) at all times. So being comfortable and on autopilot is never an option. Whether you are a solopreneur with a team of one or you have a massive team, stay vigilant in taking the pulse of your team (and self). Set your expectations in pursuit of a collective goal and find a mentor.

Pay attention to how you're showing up as well. Self assess and ask for feedback regularly because he who is not open to feedback is not open to growth. Obviously, you want to ask for feedback from people who are in the arena with you. Not those in nosebleed seats. Even if you're doing great things, there is always room for progress and you can't expect your team to make changes if you're not making any. Your self-improvement will inspire others to do the same, and will also make you relatable. If serving people is beneath you, then leadership is beyond you.

If there is a big difference between how you are

perceiving yourself as a leader and the constructive feedback you are receiving then take action to adjust. Defensiveness only slows you down. Adrenaline spikes, you get lost in your head, and you can't make fully empowered decisions. Knowing your core values and setting your intention daily on the actions you need to take to be the type of leader you see in your head drastically elevates leadership skills.

Your perception of self will align with your actions once you put in the daily practice of doing the do. Sometimes, the new action is listening more. Show up and command the day and when the shit hits the fan, you gotta keep showing up! How you show up determines who shows up. If you are a yes woman, and you are constantly seeking approval or disappointed that you are not getting compensated for your effort, take an objective look at why you do what you do. Be honest, real, and clear with how serious you are about changing. Love Punch: letting go of entitlement is hard. But being willing to say no to situations that do not serve your core values shouldn't be. Integrity should trump all so choose your hard. Leadership is not a title, it's a state of mind. Alexa, play "Boss Ass Bitch" by Ptaf.

Along with your weaknesses, you need to also know your strengths. The book *StrengthsFinder 2.0* offers a fantastic online test, and I highly recommend taking it to find your true strengths. I took the test and my number one strength is ideation. I love the creation, an idea and its point of conception. I love to watch it fly for the first time. It's that ember carrier part of me. Knowing that about myself is useful because I position myself to be very involved in that phase of a project. I also love using systems, but I realized that creating them is not where my strength really lies. I used to mentally beat myself up over this before I valued the power of working in my strengths. I would spend so much time comparing where I felt weak to other's strengths. Now, I do not feel intimidated by this. I seek people who have strengths that are opposite of mine. Together, this is how to collaborate and conquer. This is smart leadership.

We create the culture we live in. I'm all about establishing new norms and new standards to serve projects and others at our highest potential. My strength, ideation, gives me a fresh perspective and makes me an early adopter of some fantastic industry disruptive platforms. Honing this strength keeps me on the leading edge right where I thrive. Know the culture you want to create by knowing your purpose, then align and persevere. If you know your strengths then you can double down on opportunities you believe are a great fit for you. This clarity will also assist in avoiding wasted time doing things that you know you cannot master. Remember the plates you're spinning? Picking up a new plate that requires your constant focus to spin it, diminishes your peripheral view ultimately risking the most important plates. We must choose our plates wisely.

Can you identify what your important plates are?

Do you know your core values and what you stand for? Get clear on your life mission before you create your business mission. Make sure what you spend your time and energy on is something that you love. What you do for work should add to your life not take from it. You might need to make some hard decisions to get your business where you know you want it to be. In the beginning, not everyone will understand you or support you. In the end, many will champion you for sticking to your vision. Whoever is the most certain person in the room wins so can we all posture the fuck up? Remember this when the stakes are high and you need to move your goal across the finish line: Posture and work ethic will make it happen. Posturing is just another way to describe confidence. Confidence meets far less resistance than doubt. I mean knowing who you are, what you stand for, your purpose, and who you are helping. If you feel like that's a lot to have to know about yourself then your life will truly never be by your own design. It's like designing your dream home and not being able to answer if you prefer a single or two-story layout.

As a wife and mother, I want to empower moms to step into their magic, too. Business clearly isn't just for men and childless women anymore. Women bring so much value to the marketplace, so don't be ashamed of putting your kids in daycare and building your dreams while your kids are young. Remember it's quality time with your kids, not quantity. That's the old culture that we're working on changing to ensure everyone has space and a platform to shine. It's not just the dads anymore who get to travel and make their mark on the world. I build with teams who want to leverage their time and income and also want to travel and live life to the fullest! They have to bring their desire to do what it takes, though. They have to put aside their previous cultural conditioning that says they should stay home with the kids or they should be doing more "nurturing" things. They have to really want to break the mold. I can't do that part for them.

Being bold and batshit passionate is my secret sauce for bold business. Did you know the definition of passion literally means suffering? Google dictionary states that passion is: "1. strong and barely controllable emotion," and "2. the suffering and death of Jesus," with "synonyms: crucifixion, pain, suffering, agony, and martyrdom."

Unleash your "barely controllable emotion" and let it have wings, Sis! Your passion is the only thing that will take you to new heights. Embrace those things you are most passionate about and see where they lead you. And the next time you proclaim your passion for something, make sure you are indeed "passionate" and not just caught up in the moment. Ask yourself what you are willing to sacrifice and/or suffer for? I'm batshit passionate about what I do. I don't dabble and neither should you. You are just wasting time and you can't buy that back.

So go ALL IN! Be passionate and relentless, or dabble and stay stuck. It's completely up to you. If you're honest with yourself, you'll see that you want to create things that matter. You want to know that a good day's work produces something worthwhile that will be part of your contribution to others and the world. Dream big, and don't let anyone stop you. But be careful not to confuse your ego with your dream.

My dear friend, Dolvett Quince, who you probably know from "The Biggest Loser" or his best selling book The 3-1-2-1 Diet, told me that your ego is simply Exiting God Out. Now doesn't that hit ya right in the chest? Building a bold business isn't about you. Doesn't that make you feel a little relieved when it comes to what to post on Instagram? You can go right ahead now and take the focus off of you. You are simply the guide in this process. The guide who is showing your consumers the path to making their lives better and easier.

Yes, you're an amazing, super talented guide but you've got to remember you're coming from a place of serving. So can you leave your ego at the door. Here's my perspective, if you're a fashion blogger, instead of posting, "Here's my favorite little black dress!" say, "Here's my favorite little black dress and five ways you can style it for just about any summer outing." See how much more helpful that is? You're selling a product or service to make someone's life better, and they need to see you are in it for them, not yourself. If potential clients see that you're in it for them, they'll trust you and will want to buy from you.

This may sound paradoxical to what I just said.

Business is not all about you but once you have that concept down, you need to toot your own horn! Show us how great your work is. Talk about all the amazing things you offer. Guide us in the direction of making our lives better! You are not bragging. You are not a narcissist. You are running a business, and the world needs to know how you can help them with the product or service you offer. So share your story and let people see how multifaceted and iconic you really are.

In order to develop your big picture, you need to make a Vision Quest map.

Cast your vision for the next ten years. What are the top three things you want to achieve?

Now shift your identity TODAY to match your ten-year goal. Put yourself in the shoes of your future self to find out what she would be like.

Ask yourself, how does that person ten years from now feel?

Allow yourself to feel those feelings as if you were already there.

To help with this task, I am providing the following as a template. Fill in your focus for these four main areas of your life. Personalize them according to where your strengths lie.

My ten year (macro, or big picture) focus:

- Building Business
- Personal Development
- Contribution
- Home Life/ Relationships

My micro list is much more detailed but it all leads back to my four ultimate goals. You must have a vision and short, mid, and long term plans. Your short term plan will get you in position to achieve your mid-term plan, and your midterm plan will get you to that final stretch for your long term plan. Your methods along the way may change but if your focus and goals remain constant, you will get there. Break it down and set micro goals for each of the four ultimate goals, and get into the nitty-gritty day to day functionality of how it will all work. Now, ask yourself what you can do today to start on the path toward a long term goal. I'll save you the suspense. The answer is to take action! Taking action will always be the answer. Do something today that makes progress. Even the seemingly smallest step in the direction of what you desire is a victory. Progress is the cure for procrastination. Alexa, play "Pure Water" by Mustard.

The bar for the human experience has been set way too low, and there is also the misconception that success can happen overnight. Working toward your goals in microwave mindset when you should be crock-potting them is a key shift. I often jokingly say, 'It's taken me twenty-three years to be an overnight success' because, in the era of the microwave, micro-nano-second mindset and our fast and furious expectations lead to disappointment and unnecessary pain. How can we model that crock-pot success? Well, we have to first acknowledge that microwave success is like winning the lottery. Most lottery winners squander their acquired fortune within five years. They don't know how to handle the money and their relationship to it because they only came upon it by chance. They still have the old behaviors and money handling mindset that kept them trading their time for dollars in the first place. That scarcity mindset that makes them afraid of losing money because they feel there isn't enough of it and makes them use fear and stress to make their money decisions. Instead of taking smart risks and investing their newfound money in themselves and their businesses, they spend it as fast as they can on things they weren't able to buy before, and before they know it, the money is gone.

Crock-pot success comes when you offer value. If you want to impact people, then impact them! Be authentic. You obviously can't be a trust fund baby trying to offer a story of rags to riches. Typically people tune into only one radio station when listening to impactpreneurs: WIIFM, or, "What's in it for me?" What are you providing them with to make them want to respect, engage, share, come back, and later purchase what you provide?

Simply provide value.

You are your greatest asset yet you might be living your life in a lack mentality. Let's get frontal on this, shall we? You haven't spent a dime on or anytime trying to elevate your mindset and wonder why you're stuck. You haven't hired a trainer or fully followed a meal plan for longer than 3 weeks and you wonder why your workouts aren't producing results? You haven't taken your significant other on a legit date and you wonder why you're disconnected? You are your greatest asset, so invest in you! Hire people to teach you what you don't know. Invest in your mind if it is not as sharp as it needs to be. Invest in your skill set if you need to be at the next level. Be specific about the tools and strategies to invest in. Make sure they are the right ones to get you where you want to be and stop saying you cannot afford them. You can find free trainings and books to get you started. Where you have the will, you will most definitely find a way.

Don't be afraid of failure. Be afraid of people who don't talk baby talk to their dogs. Now that's crazy! Maybe you're fearful of success? Fear of success is just as strong as fear of failure. Why do you think most professional athletes make millions and end up losing it all within ten years after they retire? Why is it common for people to squander their lottery winnings? They cannot handle every limiting belief about themselves being challenged all at once. Every definition of who they believe they are and rules they have lived by has to change to meet the new quality of their new life. Most people become too afraid to look within because they see their flaws as weakness on their soul instead of normal human traits that can be changed.

Another thing people do to sabotage their shift is compare themselves to others. This negative and unnecessary practice will literally rob you at every milestone. I've learned a few techniques to combat comparison:

1. Consume less outside content. Open some time and space in your mind to create your flow by filling it less with the garbage around you. Sometimes other people's content seeps in and you start to believe that's what you should be creating.

2. Remind yourself you're not for everyone and everyone is not for you. Concentrate on connecting with those who already love your content instead of trying to get more followers.

3. Get to know who you are in your business. When you are comfortable with who you are and really get to know yourself, you'll find it's natural that you don't compare. Instead of seeing others' views as a standard to go by, you'll see them as merely a different path that they are on.

Bold business requires you to take action. Period. You can't just want it, wish for it, pray for it, meditate on it, or even rub your crystals about it. Taking bold action with the steps above will help you shift from business-woman to impactpreneur. From side gig to next level income.

- Cast your vision for the next ten years. What are the top three things you want to achieve?

- How does that person ten years from now feel?

If your partner isn't enriching your life emotionally, spiritually, or financially, having sex with them will not increase their value.

-Lindsey

7

COUNT ORGASMS, NOT CALORIES

Oh no she didn't?! Oh yes I did, Sis! Can I get an AMEN? Like, you are probably smiling that I'm being so nonchalant about orgasms, but my mother never told me about this pleasure principle so I wanted to come out the gate swinging on this. My mama was always worried about the things I let fly out of my mouth. She often said, "You kiss your mother with that mouth?", when I would casually rattle off something crude or blush-worthy. So I often had a field day with this.

In my mid-twenties, when we didn't have texting and had to actually call people on our cell phones, I programmed her ringtone to the Divinyls, "I Touch Myself" just for funsies. She would blush and laugh... Every. Single. Time. Now, in defense of my parents, they never spoke like that. Not in front of me, anyhow. I'm fairly certain it was all my time spent with my mom's bestie, Patti, that inspired my uncensored personality. My mother, originally from Oklahoma with her southern grace, would giggle when the topic of sex came into the conversation. It wasn't something she was raised to speak freely about. I chalk it up to the era of when she was born, her family dynamic, love of Jesus and her classy demeanor. What I now know for sure to be the root of her shyness is that she wasn't comfortable in her own skin. And that didn't teach me to be comfortable in mine. So, let's be transparent, you can be a lady in the streets and a freak in the sheets and that doesn't make you less classy, it makes you human.

Beyond the act of sex, the talk of maturing, developing breasts, and starting periods weren't discussed either. I was at my best friend's house the summer before eighth grade when I started my period. I called my sister at home to have her tell mom for me. It's not that my mother wasn't loving or empathetic, in fact, empathy is her number one strength. I just felt awkward to talk to my mom about it. Yet, I could talk to my friends' moms more openly and often did just that. I can honestly say that as I started my own family, my mom and I became extremely close. But we still never talked about periods, menopause or mammograms. She was there when I delivered every single baby and tradition was that she gave them their first full bath. Before my mom got sick, she had her Gigi role on lock. She really made her grandkids feel special. All I choose to do is keep close to my heart all the best moments with my mom while creating new levels of communication with my children that I, myself, didn't receive from her.

One thing I've changed with my own daughters is that we celebrated their periods. It is not a hush situation around the house. Although Maryn is more reserved and quiet, she will speak her needs while her older sister, Bella, will tell her dad that she has cramps and needs chocolate. This is the open dialogue I wanted when I was a teen. So I have created it in my home. What I wish my mom would have reinforced was to be confident with my changing body. That periods are normal and how to navigate through pads and tampons. Ya know, all the girl stuff!

I was not an overweight child, but I was thicker than many of my friends and I was conscious of it daily. I remember being so uncomfortable when it was time to get measured for costumes in dance class. In my mind, I would orchestrate how I was being judged for my costume size. I was nine years old and worrying about this shit. I danced at a studio not in my home town, and more often than not, I was the youngest one in class. I felt so inadequate with my full lower jaw, rounded belly, and thong leotard. Yes, that was the style in the late 80's.

I remember telling my mom that my hanging jawline really bothered me. I was in sixth grade and very aware of it. This is where my mom's "fixer" mentality came into play. She told me to simply keep my tongue pressed to the roof of my mouth to help lift that hanging skin. Lo and behold, she was right! It made a difference then and I often find myself still doing it out of nervous habit thirty years later. What I am choosing to now learn from it as a mother, is to fix less and affirm more.

I know my mom had the best intentions and having the same build, face structure, and hanging jawline, she would often criticize her own looks in front of me. Meanwhile, I idolized her beauty. She just wanted to help "fix" me, but what I really needed was her to affirm how I looked. Her reminders to "suck it in" so my belly didn't poke out and other, now subconscious, helpful critiques in my childhood really became the foundation of my inner critic. What I've shifted with my children is that I consciously tell them how strong, special and beautiful their bodies are. Not for vanity but for affirmation and confidence. Becoming a dance teacher, my keen eye for lines was a positive skill when I picked apart and perfected routines, but it also made me ten times more harsh on myself. I gave grace to all my dancers and saw their talent beyond their measurements but couldn't extend that same grace to myself.

What I wish I knew then that I do know now is that my body is a miraculous vessel. I was very active in sports and dance and was rarely sick. I was also fortunate to grow, birth, and nourish five babies. I had no true appreciation for what my body could do and I also had no idea it was also made for having pleasure. The only sex talk I ever received was when my parents referenced a friend in high school who was pregnant and said, "Don't be like her." Yes, that was my sex ed 101 from the parentals. No cable TV with rated R movies or MTV with Yo MTV Rap was played in my home. Yet, somehow, I knew all the movies and all the dirty songs, because that's what curious kids do. They find a way.

This is where shifting needs to take place. We shouldn't be ashamed of our bodies, our curiosity, the act of pleasure. Or the mere desire to have it. We need to stop using sex as control over our partner and sabotaging our own needs in the process. We need to wake up to the fact that our kids have access to hardcore porn on Instagram or can basically google nude pictures with internet access. I want to be my kids go-to for their questions. It's not comfortable for me but it's also my job to educate them rather than instill fear. We have to give them answers and address this because we have been generationally conditioned to suppress our needs as women and to focus on our bodies as vessels of service for others rather than for receiving pleasure.

Now, I'm pretty sure you are auditing my words with your own perspective. Maybe you don't like the fact that I have five children and just think I'm someone who doesn't believe in birth control. Or that I just like sex. You are so far in left field, Sis. However, you may be twice divorced or feel unlucky in relationships so this is no way a chapter to make you question your current situation or make you feel shame for your past. But only to show what is possible. Now there are things in my life that I'm proud of. My marriage is one of them. Let me give you a snapshot.

Mike and I met the first day of high school. A mutual friend offered up Mike's vehicle to ride to lunch in. I was fourteen. Mike was sixteen. Within six weeks, we were dating. Nine years later, we married. We wanted a large family and that's what we have. We wanted to do life our own way, and that's what we continue to do today. Our marriage is our priority and comes first. Over our children? Yes! I know that sounds unmotherly but for you young mamas reading this, your babies are your priority now (which they should be). I nursed all five of my babies each for a year. That in itself was a full-time job. Ardyn, my last baby, for eighteen months. Babies will consume you and need your full attention, and that is your season. Remember, as your babies grow into adults, they move out. Guess who you are left with? Your husband. So make sure you keep that relationship fed and nurtured along with your babies. Remember those spinning plates I talked about earlier? You must make sure that one plate is for your children and a separate plate goes for your spouse.

For my single pals, know that each encounter you have is exchanging lasting energy with that person. Your sexual partner(s) are your business but make sure it's on your terms. Your needs being met is priority. Do not settle for being someone's booty call. Now, don't get in a tizzy because I said in the chapter title to count the orgasms and now I'm telling you not to or to be picky. You are picky about what you eat, who cuts your hair and does your nails. Let's include sexual partners on this list. Women as a collective have really been stepping up their game about being vocal about their needs. We need to make sure that no one is left behind, especially our daughters.

I want my daughters to know that sex changes the relationship. It deepens the connection for sure, but you also become more attached to their partner's spinning plates, their insecurities, their feelings of lack, and their family life. Understanding your own baggage and working on your healing is hard. Adding a partner with a cluster of issues to your spinning plates makes it harder. Your partner needs to be just that, a partner. It's a mutual decision that you make for yourself. Never to say yes when you really mean NO. Your partner isn't there to make you happy. You aren't there to be their mother either. "Here's a word to my ladies, don't you give these N****** none, if they can't make you richer, they can't make you come." - Cardi B.

Riches don't have to refer to money; it's values, integrity, security, and joy added to your life. If your partner isn't enriching your life emotionally, spiritually, or financially, you'd best be certain that having sex with them will not increase their value. For many, sex is control. You must shift this mindset that control equates power to the art of pleasure and being in the moment. Love Punch: when you feel that you are servicing your spouse rather than connecting with them, you take the pleasure away and make it a job. Who wins here? No one.

Having been with Mike for more than half my life, I know that you cannot change another person. You can only change yourself. And if you cannot communicate your true feelings with a person who you're having sex with and/or says they love you, that is not a healthy relationship. Your partner is not a mind reader. Neither are you. Sitting and waiting for your partner to check in with your feelings when they have their own plates spinning will often keep you disappointed.

And if you are withholding sex as punishment or to win an argument, Sis, you are just playing yourself. I watched my mom ignore my dad whenever she was angry and I found myself as a married woman doing the same. I had to shift this behavior and learn to "take out the trash" in my marriage. If you can learn this simple shift, you will spend less nights crying yourself to sleep.

I received great advice about marriage from two people in my life. Mavis, my pastor's wife was at my home for lunch one day and told me how they have a "take out the trash" date night once a month. Meaning they specifically discuss frustrations while on their date, in a public place, so that it remains conversational and civil. Sometimes, people assume that because I am so blunt in my delivery of speech that I must treat my husband the same way. This is false. If I come at my husband like a crazy person, that's how he will perceive me and react as such. Empowerment to me does not equal a clenched fist. It's gathering your composure and thoughts to address the issue together rather than placing blame.

Walk and talks have been the most rewarding practice of taking out the trash for Mike and I. Taking an hour-long walk at night to just be alone, talk about the kids' schedules, current affairs in our businesses, and also our feelings. We've both had some incredible breakthroughs while on these walks. Sometimes we say very little and walk to just be in the moment and enjoy the sunset. Other times, it's planning out recital production, our schedules for next week or brain dumps on plans for new season at the studio. Now this is a real as it gets. Marriage is doing life with a person through good times, stressful times, sickness, and all the feels in between. There are times that I find myself being petty and withholding my attention, giving Mike a side eye but I know that I'm his one and only as he fiercely is my protector and best friend. I may threaten to "Gone Girl" him when I have to listen to his teeth scrape the fork while he eats; but hey, I never said I was a perfect wife.

I grew up in a home where my parents never fought. So, unlike many of my friends who were raised with parents who fought, this was foreign to me. What I've learned to do is fight fair and speak from a place of how I feel rather than blame. I've learned how to say how I feel when I'm upset and not to feel inferior when doing so. Feeling the strength that speaking my truth actually brings is freedom. Holding onto grudges is like drinking poison and waiting for it to hurt the other person. Mike is not only my husband, but also my partner in business, my partner in raising our children, and the person I can be the most vulnerable with. He has to be all these things or it just doesn't work. Using a rose-colored lens and expecting less from your spouse who cannot meet you halfway in all areas of the partnership (even when they are good at one thing like sex or his income) says more about you than him. Sister, set your standard and then add tax. But let's not forget to add up what you bring to the relationship also. It's a partnership.

My mama never told me that as women get older, their confidence and sex drive peaks. Most often, the male sex drive plateaus. Sometimes, it even drops. All you thirty-somethings listen up. The shift is coming!!!! That man you married, who didn't communicate love unless it was through sex, rocking all the testosterone, will soon become your prey rather than your usual predator. You are approaching your peak and feeling frustrated and rejected because of the shift in behavior. Do you see how communication in your relationship is vital? Mother nature has a sense of humor! So here you are in a new age of desire, and your husband who couldn't keep his hands off you is no longer needing the physical touch like before—this is when many women start looking outside their marriage for attention. Human behavior is not complicated. We make it complicated. We also make our desire for sexual pleasure a taboo thing and it shouldn't be. Time to shift that by less bitching to your friends and more open dialogue to your spouse on how you feel and what you want. Alexa, play "My Neck. My Back" by Khia.

The other impactful piece of advice I received was from my high school dance teacher and family friend. Sheri also married her high school sweetheart. At a mutual friend's wedding, she said that the biggest mistake young couples make is continuing the same childish behavior as married adults. By not allowing each person to individually grow into who they were meant to be, a major growth apart can occur. I took this advice as her lesson learned through experience and as my gift for prevention. Giving my husband the space to grow into the man he wanted to be allowed him to mature and become an even better version of the man I married. He does the exact same for me. Your marriage needs to grow as you grow, give as well as receive and trust. Fear is the opposite of love, and nothing can grow in its presence. Fearing change that may cause a divorce isn't the problem. Not changing for fear to evolve is the problem. I'm telling you, Sis, if you encourage your partner's growth and make some of your own as well, the two of you will mature individually yet cohesively together. Your marriage will be stronger for it. My marriage has thrived because of this.

My shift towards a positive body image has been a

long road. Because of how we've been culturally biased to hate and compare our bodies, we, women, should be unified in celebrating our bodies rather than punishing or critiquing ourselves and others for being who we are and expressing sexual desire. We should be counting orgasms rather than calories. We should be striving to have mind-blowing sex with the lights on, on top of the sheets. We should have a connection to our partner that gives us chills when we think about yesterday's love-making. We should also drop the notion that we are naughty for doing so.

If your only desire for sex is sparked when you want to have a baby, you need to shift your perception from your role as a mother to a soul in a human body having a human experience. It's not complicated but here we are, getting so uncomfortable about human nature because we've been wired to reject it from what our moms and grandmothers experienced. Until we collectively shift and share this enlightenment with our daughters, while teaching our sons that pornography isn't lovemaking, we will continue the cycle, continue the taboo and continue down a path of failed relationships. I am not Dr. Ruth or a sex therapist, but I am to my friends. Since we are now soul sisters, take this advice like you would from your bestie. More is coming and I want you to pay close attention.

Sex is exchanging energy with another person. It's taking your vulnerability to be intimate with someone else, and empowering you as well as strengthening your immune system, according to WebMD (https://www.webmd.com/sex-relation-ships/guide/sex-and-health#1, March 2019). Sex should not be labeled immoral nor should it only serve a singular purpose of procreation. We are multifaceted beings, and along with all the other things we do in life, sex is also multipurpose. I can be a nurturing mom and a whorish wife. My desire for pleasure doesn't define my morality, it makes me human. Every time you suppress your desire to express your sexual needs, you are smothering that inner fire, devaluing yourself and your humanity. You would be so pissed if your bestie never spoke her truth or saw her value in her romantic relationship. Yet here you are, lump in your throat because you know you need to shift. Yet you remain still. This is your sign, this is your wake up call to quit the shit, set your standard, and speak what you seek; unapologetically, relentlessly until attained. No guilt required!

For those that like case studies, know it has been proven that cuddling and other human intimacy actions like sex reduce stress. In *Maslow's Hierarchy of Needs* by Saul McLeod, the five basic needs for human survival are:

- Air - One of the most basic elements essential to humans
- Water - The most essential element to creating and sustaining life

- Food - The body can survive for a time without it but it's still essential
- Shelter – Protects our bodies from the harsh elements and helps us sustain life for longer
- Love & Connection – Without these, we don't have a sense of purpose
- Other physiological needs such as clothing, sex, and sleep - If these needs are not satisfied the human body cannot function optimally

Check out more at:

https://www.simplypsychology.org/maslow.html

I don't think most people realize how important healthy sexuality is. It may not be an essential element for survival (aside from the reproduction aspect), but it helps us function at a higher level. It's a pure form of connectedness and intimacy in a world that is often polarized and deemed vulgar or repressive. You will not achieve your higher purpose if you have the noise of sexual repression screaming at you all the time. It is a need that you must take care of just like sleeping and eating. Make the shift to consciously speak your desires and never be ashamed of pleasure.

You can change your mind and be unapologetic AF.

-Lindsey

8

WHAT WILL THEY THINK?

"If someone's opinion has the power to take you off course, just make sure they are paying your bills ten years from today, because they just stole your future." -Gabriel Sedlak

Hello, my name is Lindsey. I'm a recovering people pleaser and I'm here to tell you how worrying about what others think can cost you personal peace and quality of life. I used to say yes to everything and immediately regret it, stressing over the follow through. For example, if I was asked to make an appearance three months out, I would dread my commitment for three months. I literally created my own personal purgatory! I was unable to stay present in the moment, always thinking of future engagements or responsibilities I committed my time to. Not wanting to let people down, I would sacrifice my own time and energy away from my babies, for others. Learning to say no without residual guilt has given me a new lease on life. It took me getting sick to draw a line in the sand so I'm pleading you do this now rather than later. Setting boundaries and releasing others' expectations and projections can give you a new lease on life. I highly recommend you try it. But be warned, it's addicting.

While in my twenties, I was very worried about what other people thought of me. I refused to admit it and just chalked it up to being responsible. For example, I would not go to clubs or parties where I might run into parents of my dancers. I worried they would see me as a partier and deem me not responsible to teach their child. I held myself to a ridiculous standard out of fear. I would even commit to outlandish requests or birthday party appearances because I felt that to be successful, you had to constantly serve people. Love punch: serving from your heart is the goal. Serving out of guilt is from your ego.

Becoming unapologetic about who I was gave me the foundation to start saying yes when I really meant it and a big, fat NO when I meant that as well. People pleasers know this scenario of saying no with ease is theoretically possible, but not very likely to happen. What I have found is that when you speak your truth, those who respect you will understand and accept your decline. There is no right or wrong way to say no. You can be loving and unapologetic at the same time. Knowing with every fiber of your being that you can say no without apologizing is the real game changer. You can say yes today and change your mind to no tomorrow. Your goal should be unwavering faith in who you are, what you stand for and how you show up. Take it or leave it attitude please! Worrying about what people may think is like having two pairs of size 8 jeans made by two different brands. The size on the tag is the same, yet it still yields two completely different fits on your butt. One pair will fit better but that doesn't make the other pair less valuable. Just like jeans, your voice and your vibe will not be the perfect fit for everyone.

In life, not everyone is going to like adore you, value or even like you. Love yourself anyway. Once you realize that others' opinions of you are none of your business, you have reached a new level of emotional strength. Congratulations!

I didn't understand projection until I was in my thirties when I had a revelation about my childhood. My close circle of friends today have beautiful souls and physique but some childhood friends very critical, speaking so ill of others so often it made me question my own value. How did I fit in? Well, I joined in on the banter but it often left me feeling judged myself. If they were so hasty to judge whoever wasn't in the room, they probably roasted me as well. This loop of insecurity and desire to fit in left me in an "Oh my god, I'm fat because I'm thirteen and not a size 2" type of body dysmorphia. Yes, it took me twenty years to realize that I wasn't "fat." It was typical behavior from junior high school girls.

I remember reading an article in an Oprah magazine in my early twenties. Oprah wrote that she is unapologetic when she changes her mind. I read that article and felt so empowered by the idea. I wondered if Oprah could do whatever the hell she wanted to do because she was a mega-mogul, but for me to be respected, I'd have to say yes to everything. I had been so worried about people liking me, body shaming, and saying yes to things that just exhausted me for so long, I just couldn't imagine changing my mind and feeling guilt on top of it all. Fast forward to now, and I can testify that anyone can change their mind at any time. If you are constantly apologizing for it, you are not respecting your boundaries. Snap out of it! After all, you are not a doctor refusing to operate on a patient with a life-threatening illness. You can change that "yes" to a "no" and the outcome won't end in death. Doing something you do not want to do is soul-crushing if left unchecked. You can change your mind and be unapologetic AF.

Honestly, what will people think? What do they think about you? Or me? We are all too busy taking care of our own stuff to think more than a couple of seconds, if that, about anybody else's behavior. I believe we make up these intense stories in our head that people are saying or thinking awful things about us. Here's what I know to be true: if you are going places, innovating, and adding value to this world, gossip just doesn't occur to you. If you have a tiny world and tiny thoughts, though, maybe you have time to gossip. I don't know, I'm theorizing here, but after all these years, I finally let it all go. All the worry of who I might be letting down in my pursuit of something not aligned with the status quo, worry of the displeasure I might face from talking too much on team zooms (I do), worry that my team might think I'm too cliche or punny when training (I am), and paranoid they think I'm too emotional (probably so). I found myself in constant limbo of badassery and junior high antics.

Do you want to set yourself up for failure? Keep holding back in fear of what others may think. I'm telling you, the energy spent in wonderment is not worth it! You will never bloom when you wait for others to water your garden. You have to be your own nourishment and have an unwavering belief in yourself because not everyone will believe in you. The only thing left to do is throw up some deuces knowing those aren't your people. I'm drawn to souls who really have something transformative, useful, or inspiring to say. I like the Emerald personalities who are calm, cool, collected and think things through. While I'm a Saphire and wild, winded from chatter and excited. Make me laugh and I'm yours forever. However, make me question your intentions and you get dropped. You have to go with your gut and if you are constantly questioning your own intention or ethics at the mercy of others, this is your red flag. Alexa! Play "My Prerogative," by Bobby Brown.

Speaking of prerogatives … Who do you find yourself really listening to when you have a conversation? Do you listen to others over your own voice? Do you listen to others only for things you can reply to? I love talking about things that really matter. When I'm listening to someone and they start to gossip about someone else, I mentally note we are on different levels. Old Lindsey might have chimed in not wanting to be left out. New Lindsey will say, "Let's talk about something real, not tear another person down." I also listen a lot more to other people now. When they are talking to me, I'm not coming up with my response or letting my mind wander. I listen because I want to understand and connect. When you experience the difference between listening to understand verses listening just to respond, I think you'll find your relationships are far more satisfying. Not rushing through conversations but connecting with other people has been a learned skill that has served me well.

People want to feel heard and appreciated. Whether it's your spouse, children, staff, team, co-worker, students or friends, connection is key. Speaking of connecting, let me ask you another question that will push the envelope further: how many times do you speak just to fill the space with your words? Not even connecting with what you're saying. Let alone the other person. There has been a huge shift for me in this department. I have had to check myself and my anxiety filled ramblings over the years. I have learned the valuable lesson that, sometimes, silence is golden. You do not have to oblige in meaningless conversation, gossip, and trivial chatter. Find friends who dream big, have goals and speak about life over things. Once you spend time with dreamers, doers, action takers, and visionaries, you will no longer make time for the energy vampires who have much to say about nothing and you won't feel the need to drivel on and on yourself.

You don't need to be accepted by everyone you meet if you already accept yourself. Self-love takes the sting out of rejection. It's time you learned to cheer yourself on. Yes, you can feel isolated and lonely when you feel unsupported. So cheer loudly for yourself. The phrase, "You'll never be a prophet in your hometown" has a lot of truth to it. Put yourself in the shoes of your former school mates. Is it possible that you were an asshole kid or hurt their feelings sophomore year? When you are expecting people to cheer you on despite their own perception of you as an awkward thirteen-year-old with braces, you are asking for a miracle because they really cannot grasp your evolution. Or, perhaps, they are really miserable in their home life and can't support you because they can barely breathe themselves. Either way, clap for your own damn self. Stop waiting for external validation from your family, friends, spouse or even worse, the social media machine.

As a child, I used a coping mechanism to gain

external praise that no longer served me. I wanted everyone to like me, but I was very shy when meeting people. So I used my innate chameleon charm to befriend people. I just blended in by finding similarities to resonate on a higher level and I became the friend they wanted me to be—a different personality for each person. I never meant to deceive, but the empath in me paralleled schizophrenic. I just wanted to find common ground to make them feel more comfortable. Meanwhile, I was utterly exhausted. Differing opinions amongst my friends would have my head spinning. It's rough finding and remaining in your own lane when you're a kid.

As an adult, it can get really uncomfortable. When you buy people's opinions, you buy their lifestyle. Stop listening to people who have the same problems as you, and start listening to people who have your solutions. If you're seeking advice from someone who isn't living the life you'd like to aspire to, it's as if you are getting medical advice from your plumber. Does your broke cousin so and so think your business is a bad idea? Interestingly enough, he will find the flaws, but not deep dive into solutions or put any stock in it. With their own advice, they have bought their broke ass lifestyle. I would recommend moving along and seeking advice from those a few steps ahead of you, or even better, thousands of steps ahead because they will save you time and money with their pioneering wisdom. Your mindset will change when you level up your circle of influence. So stop working so hard to make others feel comfortable. Be yourself and let them raise up to match your vibes or work themselves out of your influence. Alexa, play "Level Up" by Ciara.

When communicating with others, you don't have to see it as a perpetual job interview. Would you feel relieved to know you are not the only imperfect person? You must be true to your core or you are simply wasting everyone's time. Whether you are the fake you or the real you, the following will still be true:

You'll always be too much for someone.

Too bold.

Too strong.

Too emotional.

Too successful.

Too confident.

Too loud.

So you might as well relax and be yourself. Refuse to shrink back despite how others react to your "too-muchness" because even that version will still be too much for someone. There is no winning when worrying about what others think. No matter what judgments they throw your way, don't you dare shrink back.

Resilience leads me back on top of my game every time I fall. My favorite type of people are those souls who didn't let the pain turn them cold. They used that pain and transmuted it to purpose for inspiring others. Your vulnerability can, ironically, make you invincible. Your raw truth is your armor and your life is the battlefield. When you are real, you are never caught off guard. There is nothing to hide so you sleep better at night. You only focus forward, never looking back. You can be all things: delicate, fragile, nurturing, and a total badass. Resilience really does feel like a superpower. Get good at taking the risk of vulnerability so you can start to build this resilience muscle.

Let whoever think whatever. People are going to make judgments, project their own insecurities, and extend their well-intentioned but worrying thoughts (like, "I'm concerned for you.") that will keep you down. Fly anyway. Their fear is not your truth. What they think doesn't matter. What you think and feel about it does.

Don't give up even when you don't know exactly where you're going.

-Lindsey

9

GROW, BABY, GROW

When you're green, you grow. When you're ripe, you rot. Think about it: to be green means to be new at something and learning as you go, which takes work. But, at least, you're growing and becoming something new. To be ripe means to be done, and all the learning and growing is over. But you stink! You're sitting in your stench and no one wants to be around you. It's our comfort zone, our safe place. We know what to do there. We feel safe and in control there. We can literally cruise control there! Just one small issue, though: everything you want in life but don't have is attainable right outside of your comfort zone where things are green and growing.

When we resist change we stagnate and use all of our energy trying to keep change from rock'n our boat. Because, let's face it, resistance feels uncomfortable and, dare I say, painful. We have programmed since birth to fear the word "no." Since you were a baby, you learned to stop in an instant by hearing the word "No". Don't believe me? A UCLA survey once reported that the average toddler hears the word "No" more than 400 times a day! You may, at first, think this must be an exaggerated figure but consider this: when we tell a toddler "No!" we usually say, "No, no, no!" That's three times in two seconds! If that child is particularly active, perhaps it's true; perhaps that child really does hear the word no hundreds of times a day. Although it's a good thing that they come to understand the meaning early -so that they can live to celebrate a second birthday- the bottom line is that toddlers from all cultures and across all timelines, learn what to do by constantly being told what not to do. Then, they grow older and they go to school and the pattern of speaking and learning is repeated. So, by the time they hit the workforce, even if they are very positive, energetic, and optimistically focused individuals, they are probably speaking with negative language throughout each and every day without even knowing it.

Even more ambitious is the aspiring entrepreneur. They muster the courage to start a side gig and often quit within the first two months from hearing the word no too many times. There is no system to measure inner strength. It's not the size of your ambition either. It's overcoming the word "No", seeking clarity and slappin' it up, flippin' it, and rubbin' it down to get that GRIT out! Alexa! Play "Do Me" by Bell Biv DeVoe.

Are you running out of ambition on this long, hard journey? Don't you dare quit! Quitting is not an option! What if your twelve-month-old decided learning to walk was too hard and quit? Have you ever seen a baby quit? Have you ever seen a baby not embrace all the love and adoration you can give them? Babies are the most resilient, driven, and attention craving little nuggets. Then they grow up being told, "No, no, no!" They grow up in schools that tell them what to think, when to play, and when to pee. Now, as they are young adults, we wonder why they are scared, why they cannot decide what they want to do with their lives, why they keep quitting when the going gets tough.

This cycle affects everyone, including you and me, Sis! It's damaging and we must undo the damage now for everyone under our care. It begins with us. If we can shift our limiting words to empowering ones, and increase our focus on encouraging and building up our strengths, then we can change the limiting "I can't" mentality and replace it with, "I can do anything I put my mind to!" Then we can turn to our kids and focus on their strengths rather than their grades. I'd love to see more lessons in empathy and kindness rather than memorization skills. I believe we can elevate the mindset that will set our kids years ahead of us. Yes, us! You have to be willing to grow yourself a little. Then nurture your child's growth alongside you. And then grow some more. It really starts with you.

Start the momentum and don't give up even when you don't know exactly where you're going. I have endured so many uncomfortable moments of just not understanding and having to hang in there until I did. I welcome growth because I'm clear that I'm making progress toward my goals, but it wasn't always this way. I get that it's uncomfortable being a novice and starting at the bottom. If I'm going all in, I must accept that I'm going to struggle and there is no way to avoid that. I must see the value and worth of the follow through, because when I am stretching into the discomfort of the unknown I am challenging myself to grow in order to meet new challenges and over-come them so I can succeed to the next level. Regen-eration is a remarkable defiance of the aging process.

On the flip side, when I am stuck in my comfort zone, I will age. Someone once said to me, "Nature abhors a no growth zone." I really resonate with this. When I take on new challenges, I am a beginner again. I am having to learn, adapt, grow, and evolve. My whole being is renewing and my energy level is unchartable. Everything about me is constantly refreshing as I strive toward my goal and it's exhilarat-ing! So perhaps the real growth, the genuine secret to sustained youth, is to learn new things, create new moments, switch up routine but never lose site of your core values. We must leave our fear of growing pains behind and go full speed ahead into our regenerative growth zone. When it feels like all this new growth is overwhelming, remind yourself that mastery takes time and practice. Be serious about it. If you limp along and you treat your business like a hobby, it is sure to pay you like one. Treat it like a profession, giving it your full attention and moving at a steady yet progressive pace, and it is bound to pay as such.

Now, I want to step into the unknown for a moment and help you embrace the vulnerability and fear of potential humiliation. Ask yourself what you've got to lose if you step outside of your comfort zone? Is the world going to end? Realistically, what's the worst that could happen? Maybe you'll run out of money if this investment doesn't turn out well. Then plan for that dreaded outcome and set aside some money to live on. Or seek a new investor. Or ask a friend if you can live with her for awhile if needed. Always have a backup plan to cushion you when you fall, but, then, get back in the game. Do whatever it takes to put your plans in action and don't dwell anymore on the negative "what if" outcomes, as they will only cause you to resist growth. You've got the worst of the unknown covered, so it's okay to let go and be vulnerable now because it means you're growing into something greater than you are today and your safety net will catch you if you fall along the way. Alexa, play "Pour it Up" by Rhianna.

Embracing my vulnerability has served me well in life. It has brought me a sense of peace that has allowed me to focus on forward motion, and I have been committed for the last seven years to be more of me today than I was yesterday. I am many years in the making and still a work in progress.

Now, isn't that a beautiful thing? To know that you're forever a work in progress, always growing and trying new ways to feel alive, and seek enlightenment? You may disagree, and think that all this change has got to be exhausting, but hear me out. I've learned a thing or two about this. When you are green and learning, you grow. You don't resist change, you embrace it, and because there is no friction between you and your momentum, you use up less energy. On the flip side, when you are ripe and feel you've done it all, you rot. You resist change because you are exhausted and want a break, but because there is friction you actually have to work harder to stay the same. You go into defensive mode and make snap judgments based on your ego, and then all your energy is wasted on stagnation.

I choose growth on the daily, and I like to share what I'm learning along the way. I'm an observer and a teacher. It helps me to lock in my progress and gain momentum. It's how I master everything I do. Benjamin Franklin was on the same page with me when he said, "Tell me and I forget. Teach me and I remember. Involve me and I learn." I know that putting lessons into action is the best way I can launch myself into youthful, regenerative bliss, and I know it will work for you, too. You've got some strength within you, if you decide to use it. Don't leave these words as thoughts in your mind to swish around and conjure up a storm. Write out a plan to put them in action, and watch what happens. Inaction will only breed more doubt, whereas action will cure it.

Refusing to take risk is another way to resist growth. Nearly everything in life is a risk. Yes, everything. Getting married, having kids, choosing a job, going to college, choosing a place to live in, starting a business, and investing. All risks! There is risk in making the decision to do something. There is also risk in deciding not to do something. Successful people learn how to take calculated risks. They know that time is the most precious commodity they have, and they also know that risk is necessary to reach any goal they have not already achieved.

Famous hip hop artist Lecrae Moore once said, "If you live for people's acceptance, you will die from their rejection." Please remember that rejection is merely redirection. I personally believe that when something is really meant to be and I take every action I can take, it will happen. The rejection redirects me to the best path to get where I need to go. If it's truly not in my best interest then the door doesn't open and I thank God for unanswered prayers and move along. I don't sit and lick my wounds and wallow. There is no time for that.

Billionaire Jack Ma was rejected from Harvard ten times. He couldn't even get a job at KFC, but he kept going. Michael Jordan was cut from the high school basketball team as a Freshman. Had he let that stop him, there would be no Air Jordans in my closet.

Rejection helps you get what you need in life, not what you want. This is a positive thing. It tests whether you are serious about your dreams. It will bring your insecurities and deep-rooted beliefs that you are not enough to the surface. As you step into who you were meant to be, you will be entrusted with more than you can handle. You will be uncomfortable as you evolve, but the lessons will be your blessings. You just have to stay grounded in your desires, committed to your growth, focused on what's important, and simply DO THE DO! It's always more powerful, influential, and persuasive to say what you do want and go after it. Stop speaking in fear and start proclaiming in faith. Stop speaking of what you lack and start speaking with gratitude for what you've got. Stop telling yourself no and start embracing the YASSS!

Aside from overcoming all the obstacles to growth, adults are hardwired. Sometimes we forget how to grow because we think we've already made it. We've hit all the milestones: turned sixteen and got our driver's license; turned eighteen and were able to vote and rent an apartment; turned twenty-one and we are headed to Vegas! So, clearly we've made it to where we were going, right? Let me tell you something, you haven't done shit. All you've done is grown to your adult size.

If you want to re-learn how to grow, look to a baby or a child for inspiration. They are growing so fast, we can barely keep clothes on them that fit. Aside from the physical aspect, their minds are like sponges soaking up all they can learn about the world. You need to turn your mind into a sponge again. Be fascinated by the world. It hasn't changed, after all, and you were once amazed by it. Go out into the world and find the treasures that will help you on your way to fulfillment. Travel, learn a new skill, take up a hobby, learn about different ways to do the mundane things, learn a new language, study a different religion and culture. Keep the fresh mindset that allows you to think outside the box. Babies don't know about the box yet. You can pretend for a time you don't know about it either, Sis! You just have to remind yourself to go back there often and re-learn how to grow.

10

Relationships require giving and
receiving in equal measure.
-Lindsey

10

IS THIS MINE?

Women seem more eager to acknowledge their empathy than men because we've been playing the nurturing roles in society for the most part of human history. Empathy can be the beacon of light to your ship. But, first, you must harness its power. Otherwise, it can be blinding. Many of us are empaths without realizing it and don't even know we are drowning in a cesspool others' emotions. Judith Orloff, M.D. states in her book *The Empath's Survival Guide: Life Strategies for Sensitive People* (Sounds True, 2017) that "the trademark of an empath is that they feel and absorb other people's emotions and/or physical symptoms because of their high sensitivities. They filter the world through their intuition and have a difficult time intellectualizing their feelings."

I can't even begin to describe how much being an empath has taught me about compassion, patience, and kindness towards myself and others. It has helped me understand suffering and the human experience as I've felt others' shame, self-hatred, rejection, and betrayal. It's surreal, captivating, and at the end of the day, beautiful to be empathic. I have been able to feel and experience so much that has served as a massive catalyst to my own evolution. Before I understood my gift, I felt my sensitivity was an anchor that held me down with such yo-yoing emotion that had me in the doctor's office begging for anti-anxiety meds. Empathy can be your anchor when you don't understand all of the emotions you feel, and furthermore, they may not even be yours. Do you cry easily at sad movies? Do you feel sick when someone tells you they are sick? Do you feel superhuman when your baby is hurt and you want to hug and kiss the pain away? You may very well be an empath. But if you're just now discovering this fact, you've got a long way to go to harnessing its power. So, let's begin.

Take it from me, I've lived with other people's feelings in my body my whole life, and I know how confusing it can be. I have absorbed so many more feelings than my own for so long that it became normalized. I could not tell where I ended and others began. I was drowning in the emotional noise of the outside world. Constantly overwhelmed, overstimulated, a psychic sponge since I was a child. No wonder I couldn't pick my favorite color, I was empathing everyone else and not attuned my myself. My most empathic female friends attract what seems to me as the most broken men looking for healing. I see them become depleted emotionally because they don't know how it happens and the cycle continues over and over until they learn how to release and shield it. Alexa! Play "No Scrubs," by TLC.

Being an empath has done a great deal of damage to my physical vessel, which is what I have been working to heal for the past five years. I would hold onto my emotions but I couldn't help but feel everyone's emotions as well. Not by choice, but because I had no idea how to stop it. I didn't understand what it was I was feeling. One minute I was giddy, feeling like Lil Wayne's "a-milli.". Then I would get random thoughts of not wanting to live. Like, what the actual fuck? I couldn't explain it and was too embarrassed to reach out for help because I knew it wasn't normal. I had an amazing life and was happy, yet these morbid thoughts would creep in. Not knowing why I felt this way or how to release it, I just prayed and prayed and prayed to God to make it stop.

Within six months, I randomly reconnected with a friend from high school. I hadn't spoken to her in fifteen years. She came over to grab a sample of the product I was newly promoting and mentioned she had to bolt because she was going to be late to her Reiki appointment. Of course, I asked what she meant, and she explained that this woman named April, who is an integrated energy healer, was helping her release traumas and helping her with back pain from years of basketball in college, and also just setting her mind right. I asked for her contact information and immediately emailed for the next available appointment. Five years later, with April's guidance, I am a Reiki practitioner. I see her monthly and Mike, who is an empath as well, works with her. Together, yet separately, we are releasing traumas and learning to shield ourselves from energy that is not in our highest good.

This work is redefining our children's future by removing traumas that keep showing up from past generations. We are constantly working on learning what makes us tick, what ticks us off, and how to clear and release the things that no longer serve us. Mother wound healing is my focus. It's the idea of dealing with the generational impact of what's been passed down emotionally, physically, and/or spiritually, also known as generational trauma. You better believe you have some of this, too! How are you healing the wounds within you? How are you embracing, forgiving, and loving the generations that came before you? When you are asleep to this concept it can all sound pretty random and sketch. But, when you are dedicated to healing without numbing your mind with alcohol or pills, and you want to go within to release old patterns and loops, you will learn very quickly that this is less woo woo and more of an awakening. Jesus is my homeboy and savior but I am also a Reiki practitioner and I rock Cardi B. This is how I roll. This is who I am.

I've spent too many years absolutely exhausted with emotional overwhelm and what people thought of me, until I learned how to embrace being highly sensitive with extra-sensory gifts. With April's guidance, I've learned how to release, ground, and heal myself of this internal torture. I was taught one powerful question that allowed me to release the energy of others. All I ask is: is this mine? This clarifying question for empaths finds a way to differentiate between self and others. With its answers, I don't have to carry the weight of the world on my shoulders anymore. Do you ever notice that sometimes when you're in a good and aligned space, your negative friends will try to make plans with you but the connection never pan outs? It's never personal. It's just energy. Your guides and angels won't let certain people get too close to you on purpose. Sometimes, your energy can merge with someone else.

Ever noticed times when you run into just the right person without planning on it? You just continually cross paths for some reason almost as if it's being orchestrated. I do notice when I am not centered, grounded, and shielded, that I do attract more challenging situations with people and experiences. But when I raise my vibration, I will repel people that once bothered me. They literally remove themselves from my life and my businesses. It's the law of attraction and your intention that you put out in the world. What you focus on, you attract. Reiki keeps me grounded and intentional about who I want to be and how I want to show up each day. It helps me to remember that no one else dictates how I feel so that when I start to become reactionary, I know I need to get re-centered. People can offer a vibration and I can choose to join them there or not. When I'm in a tail-spin or feeling anxious, I ask myself, "Is this mine?" I will muscle test (kinesthetic testing), and if my body rocks back it's not mine and I need to release it. If my body leans forward, it is mine and I need to address it. Here are the steps I take:

- Ground
- Center
- Shield

If you would like me to show you how I do it, go to lindseycurryshift.com and download my free video on releasing emotion.

I like to think of myself as a Care Bear doing the "Care Bear Stare," having a beam of light coming from my belly radiating my energy and light to all. However, not everyone wants my energy or light. I really respect our sovereignty and this doesn't replace my love of the Holy Spirit. This practice of Reiki has helped me find my voice, has helped my chronic anxiety, and has helped me heal symptoms of an autoimmune disease. I am passionate about sharing my journey on this awakening because I know so many people just want to understand more of what they're going through and how to make it feel better than it's felt in the past.

Being an empath left me feeling fragile and questioning my value as a businesswoman and leader, but once I learned to harness and go within, I became powerful beyond measure. Now, this doesn't mean I can shield everything. I have my moments and melt-downs but because I know how to ground, center, and shield myself, I can re-center and regain my sense of normalcy again.

Tools for grounding, centering, and shielding:

Ask that your boundaries be re-established. Affirm that you are home in your body.

- In breath: *I draw in everything I need.*
- Out breath: *I release any and all energy that does not belong to me.*

We must have boundaries in order to shield ourselves from the negative energy that some people are emanating. What are we doing spending time with people who drain us? I hate to break the news, but most often, the people who are the biggest drain on you are actually your close friends and relatives. Setting boundaries with friends and acquaintances is easier than with family because, let's face it, you are stuck with family on your most special days when you're celebrating something whether they deserve to be in your presence or not. It's a very uncomfortable feeling when you dread to be with family during special times. It's even worse to not address it or allow it to continue. I know you are reading this and thinking there's no way you can not invite your crazy aunt over for Thanksgiving. It's like, you'd have to have an uncomfortable conversation and express how you feel and she makes the best pecan pie anyhow, so you endure her craziness.

Talking about your boundaries with other people is the healthiest way to deal with a breach. Sometimes all it takes is some loving communication. But I get it, not all conversations go as planned. Sometimes, you're left scratching your head afterward going, what just happened? It's ok if this happens once in a blue moon, and you'll be able to figure out the problem eventually. But if you have a relationship where the other person is constantly leaving you feeling confused and it is a pattern that keeps happening, then they are not respecting your boundaries and will not no matter what you do. You need to get away from them safely because this is a sign of abuse. Especially if it is your spouse we're talking about. Please get professional help before you do anything drastic or say anything to them. Go to a counselor or social worker who specializes in domestic violence. And no, it doesn't have to be physical to be violent. There is a thing called violent communication, and when someone communicates over and over that they don't respect your boundaries, they are being violent towards you. With the right help, you can make a plan to get safely out of your situation.

Back to your relatives who don't live with you. There is an easier solution. Many people just spend weeks stressing over how interactions will happen during holidays, birthdays, etc. The worry of the unknown is keeping them from everyday life. Having an uncomfortable conversation is worth your inner peace rather than stewing on "what-ifs" for weeks prior to the event. I think we should consider breaking the cycle of dreading the holidays because we don't like particular family dynamics. Can we ditch the notion that blood neutralizes boundaries? That's like staying in an abusive relationship because you don't believe in divorce. I have disinvited family members from our holidays in my home and it was very uncomfortable, but my inner peace was screaming at me, "Be in alignment with your feelings". If I'm to prep, cook, and host a dinner at my house on Christmas and I do not feel comfortable in your presence, you are not invited. I don't give a shit if we are blood or bound by it. If you give me bad vibes, I cannot have you in my home. These are healthy boundaries, folks. If I can set them, we all can.

Boundaries are beautiful when you are establishing the environment that you feel is best for yourself. Boundary setting is not meant to make you a giver or taker in any situation, you are simply stating your needs and ensuring that others take note and follow through. So often we fall into the role of givers or takers in our relationships and we feel we must not break our obligation to give what someone else needs or to take what we've always been allowed to take. Most of my close friends struggle with giving too much of themselves. It is something I've struggled with as well. I have come to understand this fact and I am still learning that I need not be either a giver or a taker.

Relationships require giving and receiving in equal measure. We must learn to keep this in check in all of our relationships with friends and family. I like to say that I am my sisters' mother, because the word "mother" encompasses so many things I want to be for her and all my sisters out there. A mother is not a pushover, a victim to being too nice or too giving. A mother is wise and evolves with her child. A mother has boundaries and understands discipline. A mother contributes but also allows freedom and marvels as her children grow. A mother does not own her child. A mother gives and sustains life. A mother allows a child's self identify. A mother nurtures in a comprehensive way.

If you're currently in a "taker" relationship mode, switch it up and kick in your motherly instincts. Find a way to give so that the relationship is more balanced, and watch the relationship blossom into something beautiful. Be like a mother and give to others, especially to your fellow sisters who need you. This year, let us redefine our friendships and constructs of sisterhood and elevate them up to something so much more. Creating friendships and relationships with equal exchange gives an empath room to breathe. If things get out of balance, you can just check in and ask if it's yours and if not, you know what to do. Ignoring your intuition is like spending holidays with people not invested in your highest good. This is the ultimate form of disrespect to Self. Address the situation, and if there is no resolve, there is no bread to be broken together. Treat your relationships like your holidays with boundaries and bountiful giving and receiving. This is what the holidays are for. Reiki is another layer of my self-discovery and personal empowerment. I pray you to keep your coffee, pelvic floor, and intuition strong, Sis. Keep your head down with your mudra hand position up and stay shieldedAF.

11

If you set the intention and take action, the magic kicks in.

-Lindsey

11

INTENTIONAL LIVING

"Life moves pretty fast. If you don't stop and look around once in a while, you could miss it." -Ferris Bueller

I woke up one day, ready to face the music. Willing to accept my husband's nudge that I'd been working harder not smarter. I didn't even know what I was doing or why I was doing it. Can you say autopilot set to grind mode? I literally lived off to do lists and carried two planners and my phone calendar to keep track of it all. I was doing a dang good job meeting deadlines and succeeding my butt off ... but I was not myself, missing out on precious time with my family, always had my head in my phone, and spending a lot of money because I didn't like what that money was representing, which was my time.

ALL MY TIME. Can you believe that?! I stopped valuing money because it wasn't worth what I was giving up. And unlike money that can be replenished, your time cannot. People think that making money will solve all their problems. Is making money bad? NO! Is it bad to love money? NOT AT ALL! Is there a way to live a life that is truly fulfilling your purpose while making great money? You bet there is! One that allows me to share what I've learned in my own experience as an entrepreneur, connect with others trying to help them figure out what their own path looks like, and giving them permission to do the things that make them come alive! I've become aware and intentional of where I'm spending my time and I found myself again. The one significant question that I keep asking myself when I find myself stressed out, is: are the things I'm doing in my life slowly killing me? Or making me come alive?! If you answer this honestly, then you can proceed to shift accordingly in the art of intentional living.

Freedom is choosing to do what you want, when you want, with whom you want. When your work is defined by your purpose, passion, and contribution to the world, you will never work another day in your life (as they say). Finding a way to add value, solve problems, and lead others with a servant's heart creates a life worth living. Being financially free allows you to circulate abundance and give at epic levels as well. Freedom is a feeling of choice. It feels like bliss, joy, happiness, and fulfillment, bottled up and ready to explode from your soul. When you feel free, you simply want to give more, serve more, spend more quality time, and have life experiences with those you love most. This feeling is why persistence through resistance was worth it for me. If the above sentences do not describe your life experience but you want them to, it's time to set the intention. Intentional living is very much on purpose. It doesn't just happen. The great news is if you set the intention and take action, the magic kicks in. Believing that the universe is completely in support of you is one of the best mindsets to have while living intentionally. Don't be a victim, thinking things happen to you and you don't know why or you can't change them. Know that once you move past the mindset of "this is happening to me" and shift it to "this is happening for me," you will begin to see less problems and more solutions.

Goals can really help you set your intentions by putting on paper or in a voice recorder what you want to achieve, and then it's solidified and out there in the universe waiting to happen. Once you send your intentions to the universe, the universe will work to make them happen. I love to set lofty goals with direct intention and watch the magic happen! I want to encourage you to set your own intentions and check in with them weekly. Tell a friend or business partner so you can have faith and take action together. The experience of being witnessed allows us to access a feeling of oneness in our lives. We are all so much more alike than different and can help each other on our journey to enlightenment.

Our sameness helps us see what we can't see in ourselves. We often overlook our flaws, but we can point them out in others just fine. Take note of what your tribe says about you because what they say may lead you to more of your truth. It's hard to be intentional when we aren't in touch with who we really are, and sometimes others bring that out of us. Being around people who truly care means they'll tell you if you're doing something that bothers them, or they'll point out the things they like in you and want to see more of. Let them bring out your truth. Be open to exploring this with people you trust.

Living intentionally allows us to also experience life more in the moment. You'll stop to smell the proverbial roses, you'll start chasing sunsets, you'll look people in the eyes and really see them. It's so easy to get so caught up in yesterday with anxiety about tomorrow that we unintentionally miss today. The crazy thing about today, or even more specifically this moment, is that life is happening right before our eyes. Our real life happens in moments. Being intentional about creating them has become a top priority for me since my mom's diagnosis. She had so many plans, dreams, and desires to travel and live a happy life.

I'm now a witness to someone I love losing their someday, losing their yesterday, and remaining only in the fleeting moment. I have found the silver lining in this painful experience because seeing the lesson rather than feeling the loss is how I've been able to cope with this situation and even muster the courage to type these words. This isn't past tense writing. This is my right now, new normal and public thankfulness to my mom for how intentional I have become. I have been very intentional for years about designing my life to fit the vision I hold in my mind. I have created my own schedule, wrote my own paychecks, and built businesses side by side with some of the greatest mentors I could ask for. I have been intentional in my marriage, making sure we have time for each other and intentional with how I raise my children. I missed something, though. Before my mom got sick I was rarely in the present moment. Everything was going right on paper and around me, except things weren't right within me. I was missing my own intention, my presence, my moment. I was literally traveling and having the most amazing experiences to just forget them, and eagerly awaiting the next trip. I had a lot of expectations and they would do me dirty every time. Alexa, play "Beautiful" by Eminem.

Expectations can be a thief of your joy. I would set an intention wrapped in an expectation and, without fail, the intention would fall apart before coming to fruition. For example, I might set the intention that we would have a family night but secretly have an expectation of exactly how it should go. Instead of enjoying everyone, I'd feel frustrated that the experience wasn't meeting my expectation. Maybe the kids were crying over losing at Uno. Or didn't want to play at all. I'd lose sight of my true intention and make the ruined moment about me. I have shifted that now. Today, I set the intention, let it flow, and enjoy the moment, only checking myself when I fall back into expectation. This mindset isn't a set it, and forget it button on a crock-pot. This is a mindful practice that requires your focus and also takes diligence to make it habitual into your internal wiring. Stop focusing on where you expected to be and put your energy into what you need to do from this moment on to make it happen.

We all have dreams and aspirations to be more, do more, and have more. The obstacle is that we have set aside our desire to find our purpose. We have grown addicted to mindless chatter, false emergencies, and the busyness of binge-watching Netflix that keeps us small. What you do daily will determine your long term success. Over time, inches become feet. Feet become yards. Yards become miles... it starts with the now. Inch by inch. And believe me when I say that there are subtle cues that let you know you are on the right track and that you are being supported by the universe. It's the little random coincidences, although I don't believe they are random at all. They are called synchronicities and they are all around us.

Ever pick up the phone to call a person and they actually just sent you a text? Have been thinking of a person you haven't seen in a long time and you coincidentally run into them at the store? These are not random. They are orchestrated by your angels and in your favor. The problem is that we remain so distracted that we miss out on these blessings. We need to keep our heads up, refocus, and be present. You will see these synchronicities if you pay attention to what life is telling you. There are always signs. Turning on your car to a song with a message that you needed to hear is less random that you'd like to believe. Seeing the same numbers on your clock or on the register at the store, such as 11:11 or $3.33 can be signs. Google it, and you'll find a meaning.

What you dream about can also be a message. For example, if you have a specific dream about work and then find yourself saying and doing the same things from your dream, and other people saying and doing exactly as they did in your dream as well (like déjà vu), it is a message. It is the universe telling you, you're on the right track and to pay attention because there will be more signs to follow. Everyone is unique so you may have some other significance in your dream that is meaningful to you or a sign that has significance to only you as you're going through your day. Pay attention. Be present and be ready for your answers because they'll come to you when you least expect them and they'll subtly point you in the direction you need to go. You must be willing to orchestrate the pieces that fit together and do the work to make shift happen.

Sometimes, we stagnate along the way. We think we're making progress, but we get used to the way things are and although we may see progress, it's slowing down. Life has a way of letting us know when this is happening; you'll have a nudging feeling that you're not doing all you can, or you'll keep hearing the same messages on the radio that are songs that stand out only to you. Whatever it is, when we are paying attention we can alter our path by intentionally changing things up to get the inspiration flowing again. I learned this lesson by booking trips to places I've not been before when I noticed a stagnation.

It started when two years in a row, my husband and I spent our anniversary in Lake Tahoe. The first year was AMAZING. The second year was ok. Reason? It was more predictable and less exciting because we had already "been there, done that." So, the following year, we went somewhere new. Mammoth. We hadn't been there in years. It was a completely fresh experience. The trip was incredible because there wasn't an expectation. I'm telling you, Sis, go somewhere new and seek that! Avoid the "deja-poo" where you've seen the same ol' shit before. So many of us are working hard towards having intentional experiences in the future. Travel is one way to do that. Make the future now. It doesn't have to be an expensive vacation, it can be as simple as a picnic in your backyard. Did you know that studies show just taking a different route home from work increases happiness? Get intentional and you will see what I mean. Whether you book a trip to see the northern lights in Iceland like I did last year or you eat at a new restaurant, make it matter.

We live in a "fast food" and "door dash" food delivery culture where most things have become very easy and, at the same time, very disconnected. No one has to cook or shop in a store anymore, and smartphones and TVs mean we don't have to converse with people while we wait in the doctor's office. We are always head down, consuming content. Being entertained. Remaining distracted. Snapchat and FaceTime have replaced physical human contact, and the average length of a YouTube video has lessened because our attention span keeps shortening. It's no wonder that when I talk about mindset and choosing thoughts and taking action, I get responses like "Yeah, well it's not easy." You're absolutely right. It's also not hard, though. It's intentional.

Every action has a reaction and every choice has a consequence (good or bad). If you keep taking the same actions, in five years, you'll find yourself wishing you took a chance. You can continue to trade your time for dollars because it's safer than feeling fear of failure or being your own boss. Or you can start a side gig, you can focus on your health and vitality, leverage your time, and learn something new. Make the shifts now and reap the benefits or lesson of the results. Life can be more than just more of the same. The point is to stop the cruise control and shift into high gear of your true intentions.

Some might say they don't want a change because the status quo is easy and who wants to work if they don't have to? Fighting symptoms of depression and detoxing takes work. Parenting takes work. Relationships take work. Quitting addiction takes work. Eating less sugar takes work. Being pregnant and giving birth takes work. In a world where companies are striving to make everything quicker and easier, we are subsequently becoming lazier. People are actually more tired when they maintain lower standards. People are exhausted from underwhelming and watching their dreams die. We are uninspired and constantly in fight or flight mode each and every day.

You can shift it all by becoming intentional about what you are allowing or creating. You don't have to grind to shine. You are better when you align and flow. Alexa, play "Better" by Khalid. You've always had the goods so it now is the time to do things even when you don't "feel" like doing them. To have a different life you must do things differently. And here's your love punch: you aren't tired, you're just uninspired.

The shift work isn't to change how people perceive you. It's shifting the perception of self.

-Lindsey

12

MAKE SHIFT HAPPEN

"The truth can set you free. But, at first, it may piss you off" - unknown

I can tell you to "be brave and bold and chase your dreams," but that's all fluff and frankly, belongs on the front of your favorite gym tank. What serves your highest good is finding your inner grit instead. Bravery gets you up and moving, but grit ensures you get back up when you are knocked off your pedestal. Grit will ensure your bounce back trajectory is far higher than the place you initially fell from. You'll get back up as quickly as you fell, and use that momentum to project yourself forward and upward. Grit is going to be the biggest middle finger to all that has held you back in the past.

You'll say you've finally had enough and say "la-la-la-la-la" to all the noise in your head while you focus on your goals. Grit is getting angry enough about the things that frustrate you to do something about them. Like finally telling your ask-hole friend to go kick rocks. Those are the people who ask for all the support and favors but are ungrateful for your time. They never take your advice anyway. Moving forward, you will channel your grit because you have treasures that are hidden inside hoping you say yes to unlocking them. Say YES! Tell your story so it can heal. Say YES to feeling uncomfortable but doing it anyway. Say YES to sitting with your grief and allowing it to flow through you. Say YES to seeking the goals that are best for you and not what is projected. Say YES to unwavering faith in ourselves to see it through. Say YES to knowing our worth and seeking zero approval from others. Say YES to seeing your beauty in the mirror every time you walk past it.

This is your time for a renaissance. It's your awakening of your higher self. A rebirth with the intention to step into your God given power.

You were meant for greatness. You may not see it right now because of where you're at in life, but you have a purpose. All you need to do is find your source. When the wind blows, you can float along with the crowd or you can go a different direction, your own direction. It may seem hard because of all the strong winds knocking you down, but don't focus on what's ahead. Focus on the now.

What you focus on expands. So focus on things that empower rather than destroy. Take a few minutes and write down who you want to be and describe the life you want to wake up in. Be as detailed as possible, and allow your dream to live and breathe. Then, put it by your bed, or as a screensaver in your phone. Write it on your bathroom mirror or leave sticky notes around the house. Put up pictures that remind you of what you want as well. This is your intention letter, and it's in full color. Read it and digest it throughout the day and say thank you often for all the great things you already have. Then keep making all the little shifts we've talked about in your daily life. You might be shocked at what takes place in the following few months.

This is work. This takes time and your intention. The universe has mysterious ways of opening doors that were once closed, and making things happen that we once thought were impossible. I would keep adding things to your intention letter as new things come to you. Make sure to go back and review to see how you once felt versus how you currently feel. If you change what you want or realize you weren't asking specific enough or in the right way, you can fine-tune your letter. An example of a message that you don't want to send to the universe would be cutting out a picture of a skinny model and then cutting out the head from one of your pictures, and gluing it to the body of the model on your vision board. Your mind will be confused when you see it every day, because that's not your body type or even your body. Nothing will happen with your weight loss or health goals because you'll be in a constant state of confusion in that area. Put up a picture of yourself when you were younger and more fit, and then your subconscious mind will know what kind of vibes to send to the universe to make the shift you desire.

Wayne Dyer said, "Believing is seeing." I want to expand on that profound statement. You might take this to mean that you have to physically see something before you can believe it. I don't think so. If you are creating a life by design, believe in what you are creating (or see it) in your mind and heart first. Then, as you take the steps and allow yourself to keep the vision, you'll finally make it tangible. How ridiculous would it be to say, "I'll believe I am rich when I see it," then promptly change nothing? That's not faith. That's tomfoolery. Don't waste your time fooling yourself with quick-wit like this. Map out your goals so you can "see" the result appearing in front of your eyes. Let's start the work to create your life by design.

You are the only one who can make this shift happen. No one else will do it for you. No one else can fix your problems, or knows what you've been through. No one else knows where you are going. You don't need anyone's approval; you can start right now to change your direction to a path that will lead to more of you and less of what people expect of you. Don't be afraid of the unknown. Or that what you discover about yourself that might be negative. The only way to a solution is through the problem. You've got to know the source of the leak to stop the flood of your basement, and so it is with your life, too. What's causing you to leak happiness? Probe a little and you will find the source. Usually, there is a leak when you don't know who you are and you seek fulfillment by following the cookie recipe that someone else made for you follow. Where do you want to be? Who do you want to be with? Ask yourself questions like these every day and soon your answer will scream at you. Go out and try new things, or do some of the things you've done that didn't suit you before, and discover what speaks to you now. Remember, there are basically two things that can change your life:

1. Something new that comes into it.
2. Something new that comes from within.

Do you want captivating friends, a happier marriage, more connection, and fulfilling relationships? Then, Sis, transform yourself first. Mothering your spouse won't make them happy. Mother yourself instead. Make the shifts in your life first and you'll see it all reflected back to you. Love punch: if you want to know what you think of yourself, then ask what you think of others because that's your answer. Sometimes, we need to see that we are the common denominator in our toxic relationship equation. Self-awareness and shifting will fix that right as rain, my love. We can shift our focus from outward to inward and how we, ourselves are the catalyst for change, flow from what's wrong and stuck to where we are perfectly imperfect and improving. It's taking baby steps versus remaining stagnant. You have to slow down to speed up.

When you slow down, you'll begin to spot more quickly and efficiently what keeps you in old, negative loops. You will identify those thought patterns and implement your newfound art of mastering your attention, creating a new intention, embracing newfound fulfillment, and an eagerness to give more forgiveness. Paying attention to what we pay attention to will lead to the heart of our self-worth, relationships, parenting, leadership, healing, and spirituality, and will help us identify any waste that needs to be eliminated. Doing things just to feel good in the moment like rushing to buy shit you don't need, drinking too much, or using people only for sexual pleasure hasn't sparked healing in the past, and it sure as hell will not help you now. Don't get me wrong—I'm all about sparking joy, but not if it keeps my emotions spiking until they eventually flatline.

Next up in your enlightenment journey is to know your circle. I'm gonna keep this short and sweet. When you share your goals, dreams, and aspirations with people who don't have any for themselves, they will be hard-pressed to support you because they are having trouble supporting themselves. Be around people who put action behind their words: the doers, the rainmakers, the people making things happen that you respect and want in your life. If you are the smartest or most successful person in your circle, get a new circle. The more you understand this, the less approval or admiration you'll need from others.

Remaining connected to your homies who continually struggle with their own insecurities will keep you seeking their approval and validations that are not necessary for your renaissance. I call this emotional purgatory. Basically, you are remaining stuck by others' sins. This doesn't mean they are unworthy of your love and friendship, but they are keeping you from your next level, Sis! Now don't be sad if I've just called out your closest friends and family. I'm sure they love you. However, they probably don't support you like you'd hoped for. Shift your focus from hanging off their every word to searching for the encouragement and examples you need in others. You might have strangers champion you more than people who've known you your whole life. Persevere anyhow. Succeed anyway. Keep showing up for you! Just seek like-minded people as you begin to shift. Your network is your net worth and waiting for the slow clap from your unmotivated peers is literally choking out your soul.

I know I keep picking at this "support from others" scab because, like a moth to a flame, the first thing we want to do when we get excited about something good in our life is tell the people closest to us. They are your friends, relatives, or co-workers. The issue I have witnessed too many times is someone who has had a breakthrough goes and tells their people about it only to be met with crickets or nay-saying, followed by the person falling right back to their same old life. Cardi B put it this way in her song called *Money*: "You know who popped the most shit? The people whose shit not together." By all means, tell your people! Share the joy. But if your people are not on the same page with you, don't you dare blink if you're on a solo mission. Great. You're not alone. I'm on your mission, too! And I want to cultivate an entire tribe of women who make shift happen every day.

At the end of the day, we all want to feel like we are enough. The challenge is that it can only come from within to really know it. So many of us fall prey to false confidence. This is when we look outside ourselves for validation and we either put down others by projecting our insecurities onto them to make ourselves look good, or we accept their projections and expectations placed on us. The shift work isn't to change how people perceive you. It's shifting the perception of self. It's how we start shifting our conditional love and acceptance to unconditional love and patience. And it's how we move from *telling* people we are strong, classy, and confident to *embodying* and *exemplifying* all these things. It's time to walk it like we talk it! Alexa, cue "Walk It Talk It," by Migos.

It all starts within and how you see yourself. You do not have to play with your friends if you don't want to. You wouldn't make your four-year-old have a playdate, or force them to hug a family member if they didn't want to. So why are you constantly writing checks your ass can't cash, remaining in toxic relationships, staying in a job you hate, keeping friends who discuss people rather than their goals, idolizing strangers on social media who encourage you to drink teas and shit yourself to be thin, remaining stuck in the "someday" I'll meet someone or travel and do things I've always wanted to do (kind of) life? Someday will never come unless you start changing your life today.

I want you to go within and find your inner five-year-old and give her the love she never got but desperately needed. Go find your inner twelve-year-old and give her the acceptance and confidence she lost when bullied in middle school. Go find your inner eighteen-year-old and give her healing grace from poor decisions made in high school. Go now! Seek the real you behind the broken smile. The one who's been in a fog, feels she is fat, ugly, unlovable, and undeserving of loyalty by men. You have so much pain that you have held onto for years and you don't dare let it go because it's become your identity. Love punch: that's not your identity. That was an experience. I'm asking you to let those negative emotions go. You cannot change the past but you are missing out on your future by not releasing the emotions that do not serve you. Constantly auditing your past will keep you there. Unless you are writing a memoir, just move along and say thank you, next. Alexa, play Ariana Grande "thank u, next."

Life happens in small fragments that we call moments. We can elevate our experience together by being fully aware and collectively create one shift at a time. You deserve a life full of joy. It's time to look within, make your divine plan and start the shift work.

HOLY SHIFT! WORKSHEET #5

- Where do you want to be?

  ....

  ....

  ....

- Who do you want to be with?

  ....

  ....

  ....

- What's stopping you?

  ....

  ....

  ....

- What's one step you can take today?

- Are you ready to take it?

Oh Snap! Here you go! *Holy Shift!* Alexa play "All I Do Is Win" by DJ Khaled.